I0166879

Stepney Parish
Records
of
Somerset County,
Maryland

Saint Bartholomew's at Green Hill

Saint Mary's at Tyaskin

Ruth T. Dryden

HERITAGE BOOKS
2008

HERITAGE BOOKS
AN IMPRINT OF HERITAGE BOOKS, INC.

Books, CDs, and more—Worldwide

For our listing of thousands of titles see our website
at
www.HeritageBooks.com

Published 2008 by
HERITAGE BOOKS, INC.
Publishing Division
100 Railroad Ave. #104
Westminster, Maryland 21157

Copyright © 1989 Ruth T. Dryden

All rights reserved. No part of this book may be reproduced or
transmitted in any form or by any means, electronic or mechanical,
including photocopying, recording or by any information storage
and retrieval system without written permission from the author,
except for the inclusion of brief quotations in a review.

International Standard Book Numbers
Paperbound: 978-1-58549-136-0
Clothbound: 978-0-7884-7018-9

STEPNEY PARISH

"At a Vestry held at Green Hill Church in Stepney parish on the fourth day of July one thousand seven hundred and thirty eight Vestrymen present the Reverend Alexander Adams, Capt. John Handy, Mr. Robert Dashiell and Mr. Mitchell Dashiell, Mr. Matthias Dashiell and Mr. Levin Dashiell Church Wardens and Day Scott Register.
Ordered by the Vestry that and Advertisement should be made upon the parrish register acquainting future ages of this service why so many persons born and married several years ago and put on Record after them that were born married or buried lately----the reason is this the people have never been made sensible of the Advantage of Recording their families till of late and therefore there have been more persons Recorded the year by past then for many years preceeding."

These records are from the register of Stepney Parish and every attempt to maintain the order and spelling of the names, as enterred, was made.

Names like Parrimore, Parmore, Talor, Taylor, Hughs and Hughes will be found in the index since that is the way they were written in the document. All of book one was in the same handwriting so errors have been found in the records. This was noted in a letter included in the Stepney Parish book written by Isaac W. K. Handy of Orange C.H. Virginia on 30 May 1866.
"Dear Sir - I thank you for yours of the 25th inst enclosing the extracts from the Records of Stepney parish. They are important to my work and you have done me a great favour. I regret that I had no apportunity of examining these records during my late visit to the E. Shore. You give me the name of John Handy who married Ann Nutter with the date of marriage Dec. 25 1748 and the birth of their son Thomas 18 March 1749. This would make his birth about three months after the marriage. Is there not a mistake in your figures as I had calculated his birth from other dates in my possession (an affidavit given in Sept. 1772 in which he says he was 23 years old) in 1750. Do you find any other notice of this Thomas Handy on the Records. You give him a son of Jas and Anne Handy, I suppose of course it is John and not Jas. in the Record. The George Handy whose family record you sent was my great grandfather and I am pleased to find that the dates correspond with dates which I already had in my possession except in the case of Elizabeth which you put down as June 8 1775. This Elizabeth was the wife of the late Dr. Saml Ker of Princess Anne. Willl you not be kind enough to refer again to the records and see whether the James Handy you sent me is not James Hardy but I have found no James Handy living at so early a period in Somerset. It is very important to setle this question and you will do me a great favour to refer very closely once more to this name. etc."

1.

STEPNEY PARISH RECORDS

Josiah COTTMAN son of Joseph and wife Hannah was born 20 March 1736

Thomas VINSON married Sarah STANFORD 18 January 1724

James VINSON son of Thomas and wife Sarah was born 13 July 1724

Elizabeth VINSON daughter of Thomas and Sarah born 10 November 1725

Mathias VINSON son of Thomas and Sarah was born 3 December 1728

Isaac VINSON son of Thomas and Sarah was born 18 July 1732

Sarah VINSON daughter of Thomas and Sarah was born 18 March 1734

Jonathan VINSON son of Thomas and Sarah was born 11 August 1736

Samuel HALL married Margrit READY 13 April 1732

Mary HALL daughter of Samuel and Margrit was born 19 March 1733

James HALL son of Samuel and Margrit was born 19 August 1735

Samuel HALL son of Samuel and Margrit was born 27 February 1736

John PARSONS married Elizabeth FALUM 3 April 1737

Falum PARSONS son of John and Elizabeth was born 17 January 1737

James PARREYMORE married Mary FRIGS 25 September 1719

William PARREYMORE son of James and Mary was born 21 December 1720

Isaac PARREYMORE son of James and Mary was born 21 February 1722

Mary PARREYMORE wife of James died 29 March 1723

James PARREYMORE, widower married Elizabeth SHEEHEE 31 January 1724

James PARREYMORE son of James and Elizabeth was born 28 January 1726

Joshua PARREYMORE son of James and Elizabeth born 20 February 1728/9

Moses PARREYMORE son of James and Elizabeth was born 1 May 1731

Arnol PARREYMORE son of James and Elizabeth was born 15 November 1733

Stevan PARREYMORE son of James and Elizabeth was born 28 November 1736

James HARDY married Elizabeth TRONE 8 May 1723

James HARDY son of James and Elizabeth was born 29 December 1723/4

Temperance HARDY daughter of James and Eliz. was born 14 July 1725

Isaac HARDY son of James and Elizabeth was born 21 July 1728

Roger HARDY son of James and Elizabeth was born 1 February 1731/2

Mary HARDY daughter of James and Elizabeth was born 29 March 1733

William HARDY son of James and Elizabeth was born 23 May 1735

William NUTTER married Elizabeth McCLESTER 22 June 1733

William NUTTER son of William and Elizabeth was born 13 November 1734

Margrit NUTTER daughter of William and Eliz. born 13 February 1736/7

William NUTTER died 17 October 1737

Peter MAGEE married Mary NOBLE 23 December 1736

Elinor MAGEE daughter of Peter was born 5 November 1737

John POWELL married Rebecah GILLIS 26 April 1737

Robert TWILLEY married Ann WEATHERLY 9 April 1732

James TWILLEY son of Robert and Ann was born 16 January 1733

Eliz TWILLEY daughter of Robert and Ann was born 9 August 1735

Robert TWILLEY son of Robert and Ann was born 20 February 1738

Thomas LANGFORD married Mary COLLINS 14 July 1723

Mary LANGFORD daughter of Thomas and Mary was born 25 June 1725

Thomas LANGFORD son of Thomas and Mary was born 15 May 1727

Sarah LANGFORD daughter of Thomas and Mary was born 19 October 1729

Ann LANGFORD daughter of Thomas and Mary was born 4 January 1732

Mary LANGFORD wife of Thomas died 3 January 1734

William LINGO son of Richard was born 9 May 1733

Richard LINGO son of Richard was born 2 September 1735

Joshua HITCH son of John and Eliz. was born 1 February 1729/30

John HITCH son of John and Eliz. was born 11 July 1732

James HITCH son of John and Eliz. was born 23 January 1734/5

Joseph HTICH son of John and Eliz. was born 13 June 1737

Thomas COX married Elizabeth CLARKSON 4 December 1714

3

Elizabeth Cox daughter of Thomas and Eliz. was born 4 December 1715

Thomas COX son of Thomas and Elizabeth was born 23 December 1717

Daniel COX son of Thomas and Elizabeth was born 29 April 1723

John COX son of Thomas and Elizabeth was born 9 August 1726

Mary COX daughter of Thomas and Elizabeth was born 22 February 1730

Sarah COX daughter of Thomas and Elizabeth was born 24 March 1733

Robert DASHIELL married Esther HARDY 16 September 1735

Jane DASHIELL daughter of Robert and Esther was born 5 May 1737

John CALLOWAY Sr. married Mary GOULD 25 December 1709

Ebenezer CALLOWAY son of John and Mary was born 24 August 1727

Sarah CALLOWAY daughter of John and Mary was born 4 October 1729

Rachell CALLOWAY daughter of John and Mary was born 28 January 1731/2

Katherine CALLOWAY daughter of John and Mary was born 26 October 1734

Nelly SHIRMAN daughter of Job was born 14 November 1736

Lowder SHIRMAN son of Job son of was born 2 February 1737

George SMITH married Judah TURNER 10 February 1730

Sarah SMITH daughter of George and Judah was born 29 November 1732

Mary SMITH daughter of George and Judah was born 15 September 1734

Archeybold SMITH son of George ad Judah was born 31 March 1736

John BRADLEY Married Margrit (qv) DEAN 4 December 1733

Betty BRADLEY daughter of John and Margrit was born 17 September 1734

Dean BRADLEY son of John and Margit was born 14 September 1736

John NEWTON married Mary _____ 20 October 1733

Betty NEWTON daughter of John and Mary was born 20 July 1734

John NEWTON son of John and Mary was born 11 August 1736

Richard HOVINGTON married Ann GARRIT 24 August 1734

John HOVINGTON son of Richard and Ann born 18 November 1734

Jonathan HOVINGTON son of Richard and Ann was born 13 January 1736

4

Alexander CARLILE married Margrit McCLESTER 6 July 1720

Adam CARLILE son of Alexander and Margit was born 13 February 1724/5

John CARLILE son of Alexander and Margit was born 28 January 1725/6

Moses DRISKELL married Katherine ELGILL 4 February 1713

Rachell DRISKELL daughter of Moses and Katherine born 20 February 1718

William DRISKELL son of Moses and Katherine was born 26 November 1719

Ann DRISKELL daughter of Moses and Katherine born 28 February 1720/1

Mary DRISKELL daughter of Moses and Katherine born 7 August 1723

Comfort DRISKELL daughter of Moses and Katherine born 5 November 1726

Moses DRISKELL son of Moses and Katherine was born 26 November 1729

Elgit DRISKELL son of Moses and Katherine was born 10 December 1736

Robert MALLONE married Mary HARRISON 12 September 1728

Eliz. MALLONE daughter of Robert and Mary was born 28 January 1729

John MALLONE son of Robert and Mary was born 19 January 1732

Sarah MALLONE daughter of Robert and Mary was born 20 July 1734

Robert MALLONE son of Robert and Mary was born 6 December 1736

John LANGFORD married Ann RALPH 24 August 1714

Jonathan LANGFORD son of John and Ann was born 11 October 1736

Thomas STOCKWELL son of George Hance and Mary was born 31 March 1731

Daniel HURT married Sarah PHILLIPS 11 February 1731

Nelly HURT daughter of Daniel and Sarah was born 10 October 1732

John HURT son of Daniel and Sarah was born 15 March 1733

Jane HURT daughter of Daniel and Sarah was born 6 August 1735

William MORE Jr. married Rachell RALPH 7 March 1732

Levin MORE son of William and Rachell was born 1 April 1733

Elizabeth MORE daughter of William and Elizabeth born 2 January 1734/5

Ralph MORE son of William Jr. and Eliz. was born 8 October 1736

William STUART married Katherine DONALDSON in 1721

5

Jane STUART daughter of William and Katherine born 10 February 1724

Katherine STUART daughter of Wm. and katherine born 20 October 1726

Agnes STUART daughter of Wm. and Katherine was born 5 December 1728

Rebecah STUART daughter of Wm. and Katherine was born 13 October 1730

William STUART son of Wm. and Katherine was born 25 December 1733

William STUART died in 1734

William HARVEY married Mary HOMES 14 October 1721

Elizabeth HARVEY daughter of Wm. and Mary was born 17 October 1726

Mary HARVEY daughter of William and Mary was born 18 July 1730

Nathaniel HARVEY son of William and Mary was born 13 April 1735

Edmund SHILES married Elinor HAINS 7 February 1733/4

Elizabeth SHILES daughter of of Edmund and Elinor born 28 August 1737

Thomas WALLER Jr. married Jane CALLOWAY 4 February 1733/4

Joshua WALLER son of Thomas and Elinor born 12 January 1734/5

Jane WALLER daughter of Thomas Jr was born 6 February 1736/7

William LANGSDALL married Judah DAW 22 August 1734

Mary LANGSDALL daughter of William and Judah was born 14 June 1735

John LANGSDALL son of William and Judah was born 6 November 1737

Mary MacDOWELL daughter of John and Mary was born 17 October 1727

Alice MacDOWELL daughter of John and Mary was born 15 March 1728

Joshua MacDOWELL son of John and Mary was born 12 August 1732

Ann MacDOWELL daughter of John and Mary was born 1 June 1736

William BROWN married Susannah CARMICHAEL 5 September 1723

Robert BROWN son ot William and Susannah was born 24 May 1724

William BROWN son of William and Susannah was born 17 July 1726

John BROWN son of William and Susannah was born 14 April 1728

Mary BROWN daughter of William and Susannah was born 2 July 1730

James BROWN son of William and Susannah was born 16 May 1732

George BROWN son of William and Susannah was born 27 May 1734

William WEATHERLY married Charrety NICHOLSON 5 April 1719

Richard WEATHERLY son of William and Charrety was born 20 March 1720

Joseph WEATHERLY son of William and Charrety born 4 January 1721/2

Charrety WEATHERLY daughter of William & Charrety born 8 July 1724

Patience WEATHERLY daughter of William & Charrety born 12 August 1726

Mary WEATHERLY daughter of William and Charrety born 21 December 1729

Elijah WEATHERLY son of William and Charrety born 23 February 1731/2

Nathaniel WEATHERLY son of Wm. and Charrety was born 31 August 1734

William WEATHERLY died 17 April 1734/5

Thomas MARVILL married Elizabeth HUGINS 1 June 1721

Abigail MARVILL daughter of Thomas and Eliz. was born 15 April 1723

Tiley Clear MARVILL daughter of Thomas & ELiz. born 4 December 1726

David MARVILL son of Thomas and Elizabeth was born 5 January 1729

Thomas MARVILL son of Thomas and Elizabeth was born 11 November 1732

Phillip MARVILL son of Thomas and Elizabeth was born 13 November 1735

Robert MARVILL son of Thomas and Elizabeth was born 15 May 1737

Hill COX married Charrety SEADY 5 January 1735/6

Jonathan HOVINGTON married Betty COOPER 10 December 1729

James HOVINGTON son of Jonathan and Betty was born 14 June 1731

Littleton HOVINGTON son of Jonathan and Betty was born 9 May 1733

Mary HOVINGTON daughter of Jonathan and Betty born 12 January 1734/5

Luke HOVINGTON son of Jonathan and Betty was born 3 February 1736/7

Joseph TULLEY married Sarah JEFFERSON December 1733

Charles TULLEY son of Joseph and Sarah was born 20 August 1736

Bryan READY married Katherine CAR 12 October 1735

William READY son of Bryan and Katherine was born 13 July 1736

Henry SPEAR married Jane CALLOWAY in 1711

John SPEAR son of Henry and Jane was born 15 February 1723

Jacob SPEAR son of Henry and Jane was born 3 March 1725

Mary SPEAR daughter of Henry and Jane was born 25 May 1727

Sarah SPEAR daughter of Henry and Jane was born 20 May 1729

Andrew SPEAR son of Henry and Jane was born 3 December 1731

Moses SPEAR son of Henry and Jane was born 1 June 1733

Aron SPEAR son of Henry and Jane was born 25 November 1734

James CATHALL son of James was born 5 April 1731

Esther CATHALL daughter of James was born 25 January 1733/4

Sarah CATHALL daughter of James was born 27 September 1737

William CALLOWAY married Margrit MORE 1 December 1734

Jane CALOWAY daughter of William was born 4 January 1735/6

Margrit CALLOWAY daughter of William and Margrit was born 7 June 1737

Margrit OLLPHINT daughter of William and Ann was born 23 April 1734

William OLLPHINT married Sarah JONES 23 February 1736

John PARSONS married Mary SMITH 3 April 1729

Peter PARSONS son of John and Mary was born 14 May 1730

Nelly PARSONS daughter of John and Mary was born 4 December 1733

John PARSONS son of John and Mary was born 11 September 1736

George PARSONS son of Joh and Mary was born 14 April 1738

Jane RIGHT daughter of William was born 2 November 1724

Beary RIGHT son of William was born 18 March 1723

Sollomon RIGHT son of William was born 2 February 1726

Charles RIGHT son of William was born 23 October 1731

Littleton RIGHT son of William was born 23 July 1734

William RIGHT died 3 April 1734

Samuel COOPER married Sarah WILSON 3 April 1722

William COOPER son of Samuel and Sarah was born 11 February 1724

Abraham COOPER son of Samuel and Sarah was born 15 November 1726

Levin COOPER son of Samuel and Sarah was born 28 March 1728

Samuel COOPER son of Samuel and Sarah was born 28 January 1733

Thomas GILLISS married Priscilla DENWOOD 22 September 1720

Levin GILLISS son of Thomas and Priscilla was born 22 August 1721

Betty GILLISS daughter of Thomas and Priscilla born 13 December 1722

Esther GILLISS daughter of Thomas and Priscilla born 6 October 1724

Leah GILLISS daughter of Thomas and Priscilla was born 1 April 1726

Betty GILLISS daughter of Thomas and Priscilla born 25 December 1727

Thomas GILLISS son of Thomas and Priscilla was born 14 November 1729

Mary GILLISS daughter of Thomas and Priscilla was born 20 July 1731

Prissee GILLISS daughter of Thomas and Priscilla born 16 March 1732/3

Sarah GILLISS daughter of Thomas and Priscilla born 26 January 1734/5

Nelley GILLISS daughter of Thomas and Priscilla born 7 October 1736

Betty GILLISS daughter of Thomas and Priscilla died 24 October 1725

John DISHROON married Francis HILL 27 October 1728

Jane DISHROON daughter of John and Francis born 2 June 1732

Margrit DISHROON daughter of John and Francis born 25 November 1735

Henry McCABE died 1 November 1731

Archibald RICHIE married Elizabeth McCABE widow, 10 April 1732

James RICHIE son of Archie and Elizabeth was born 2 April 1738

John GOSSLEY married Joanah CHEESEMAN 6 June 1734

Esther GOSSLEY daughter of John and Joanah was born 22 March 1734/5

Leah GOSSLEY daughter of John and Joanah was born 1 February 1736/7

Charles DASHIELL married Elizabeth BALLARD 1 January 17323

John DASHIELL son of Charles and Elizabeth was born 18 December 1734

Levin DASHIELL son of Charles and Elizabeth was born 7 October 1736

John MORE son of William and Rachell was born 27 July 1738

9

Benjamin DASHIELL son of Col. George and Eliz. born 5 January 1738/9

Joseph ROBERTSON son of John and Eliz. died 21 December 1738

Sarah BORDMAN daughter of Francis and Sarah was born 6 October 1725

Arthur WEATHERLY son of John and Jane was born 13 March 1738

Day SCOTT married Alice BALLARD 20 February 1728

Betty Day SCOTT daughter of Day and Alice was born 7 December 1731

Edward Day SCOTT son of Day and ALice was born 14 March 1734

Edward Day SCOTT son of Day and Alice died 28 May 1734

Mary Day SCOTT daughter of Day and Alice was born 10 April 1735

George Day SCOTT son of Day and Alice was born 15 March 1736

John MERICK son of Isaac and Sarah 10 December 1727

Luke MERICK son of Isaac and Sarah was born 6 January 1731

George MERICK son of Isaac and Sarah was born 5 December 1733

Isaac MERICK son of Isaac and Sarah was born 25 August 1736

Nehemiah MERICK son of Isaac and Sarah was born 12 April 1738

Mary CAWDRY daughter of Abraham and Martha was born 14 April 1738

Isaac STEVENS married Ann ROE 26 October 1723

Rebecah STEVANS daughter of Isaac and Ann was born 7 August 1727

William SULLIVAN married Margrit NOBLE 28 March 1722

Mary SULLIVAN daughter of William and Margrit born 17 April 1724

Sarah SULLIVAN daughter of William and Margrit was born 2 April 1726

William SULLIVAN son of William and Margrit was born 19 September 1729

Leah SULLIVAN daughter of William and Margrit was born 12 April 1731

John SULLIVAN son of William and Margrit born 4 February 1733/4

Judah WILLIAMS daughter of Richard and Susanah born 23 August 1730

Susannah WILLIAMS daughter of Richard and Susanah born 5 April 1735

Thomas SHIRMAN married Rachel COLLINS 20 February 1736/7

Susanah SHIRMAN daughter of Thomas and Rachel born 22 December 1737

Richard STEVANS married Rachel HACKER 25 December 1730

Nelly STEVANS daughter of Richard and Rachel born 28 October 1731

Mary Hacker STEVANS daughter of Richard & Rachel born 28 Dec. 1733

Stevan STEVANS son of Richard and Rachel was born 1 August 1735

John DISHEROON Jr. married Mary _____ 21 December 1732

Obediah DISHEROON son of John and Mary born 21 January 1733

Steven DISHEROON son of John and Mary born 9 July 1736

John JONES married Ann CARTER 10 July 1723

Ezekiel JONES son of John and Ann was born 8 June 1724

Mary JONES daughter of John and Ann was born 2 September 1726

Sarah JONES daughter of John and Ann was born 10 August 1728

Elizabeth JONES daughter of John and Ann was born 5 February 1730

Ann JONES daughter of John and Ann was born 28 May 1733

Charety JONES daughter of John and Ann was born 11 August 1736

Alexander THORNS married Charety SHIRMAN widow, 10 October 1726

Jacob THORNS son of Alexander and Charety was born 22 January 1729

Anne THORNS daughter of Alexander and Charety was born 8 June 1734

Thomas THORNS son of Alexander and Charety 27 March 1735

Edmund THORNS son of Edward and Ann was born 18 August 1732

Dorothy TULLEY daughter of Stevan Jr. and Katherine born 29 May 1738

Ann POTTER daughter of Joseph and Ann was born 2 April 1734

Sarah POTTER daughter of Joseph and Ann was born 8 November 1736

Elizabeth DISHEROON daughter of John & Frances was born 13 June 1738

Stevan HOPKINS son of Stevan and Elizabeth was born 28 May 1732

Martha HOPKINS daughter of Stevan & Eliz. was born 28 February 1733/4

Robert HOPKINS son of Stevan and ELizabeth was born 28 June 1736

Charles HOPKINS son of Stevan & Elizabeth was born 1 January 1737/8

Thomas LARREYMORE son of Thomas & Judith was born 21 February 1734.

11

Betty LARREYMORE daughter of Thomas and Judith born 10 March 1738

John RHODES married Sarah MOORE 21 September 1735

Mary RHODES daughter of John and Sarah was born 18 July 1736

John RHODES son of John and Sarah was born 20 February 1737

Thomas BOWLIN married Margery RUARK 6 January 1731/2

Margrit BOWLIN daughter of Thomas and Margery was born 1 October 1732

Mary BOWLIN daughter of Thomas and Margery was born 6 January 1731/2

John WOOLLON married Margrit DAVIS 10 March 1726

Sarah WOOLLON daughter of John and Margrit was born 27 October 1729

Margrit WOOLLON daughter of John and Margrit was born October 1731

Elizabeth WOOLLON daughter of John and Margrit was born 20 July 1733

Benjamin WOOLLON son of John and Margrit was born 3 December 1736

William SHOCKLEY son of David was born 4 August 1719

Mary SHOCKLEY daughter of David was born 13 November 1723

Solomon SHOCKLEY son of David was born 6 December 1726

Sarah SHOCKLEY daughter of David was born 13 January 1728

Benjamin SHOCKLEY son of David was born 4 July 1731

Isaac SHOCKLEY son of David was born 1 November 1736

Richard SHOCKLEY married Sarah TODVINE 19 October 1736

Saborah SHOCKLEY daughter of Richard and Sarah was born 29 July 1737

Sarah GILLISS daughter of John and Margrit was born 20 June 1721

John GILLISS son of John and Margrit was born 5 August 1723

Betty GILLISS daughter of John and Margrit was born 25 May 1725

Bridgit GILLISS daughter of John and Margrit was born 26 April 1729

Joseph GILLISS son of John and Margrit was born 27 April 1732

Ann WINSOR daughter of Johna and Ann was born 15 March 1718

Sarah WINSOR daughter of John and Ann was born 4 April 1720

Rachell WINSOR daughter of John and Ann was born 13 March 1722

John WINSOR son of John and Ann was born 22 January 1725

Prisilah WINSOR daughter of John and Ann was born 29 February 1727

James WINSOR son of John and Ann was born 22 September 1729

Charety WINSOR daughter of John and Ann was born 29 April 1731

Alice WINSOR daughter of John and Ann was born 10 April 1733

Joseph WINSOR son of John and Ann was born 19 July 1736

John WINSOR died 14 November 1737

Lewis DISHROON Sr. married Jane COX 20 November 1703

John DISHROON son of Lewis and Jane was born 6 October 1704

Levin DISHROON son of Lewis and Jane was born 28 May 1707

Thomas COVINGTON married Mary FILLET 20 August 1731

Ann COVINGTON daughter of Thomas and Mary was born 24 May 1732

Levin COVINGTON son of Thomas and Mary was born 14 August 1734

Priscilah COVINGTON daughter of Thomas and Mary born 18 September 1736

Isaac COOPER married Tabitha MILLBY 22 February 1731

Ann COOPER daughter of Isaac and Tabitha was born 24 May 1733

Mary COOPER daughter of Isaac and Tabitha was born 24 April 1735

John COOPER son of Isaac and Tabitha was born 29 October 1737

John COOPER son of Isaac died the same day 29 October 1737

Sarah HOVINGTON wife of Thomas died 25 November 1726

Thomas HOVINGTON married Margrit EVAINS 11 August 1727

Richard HOVINGTON son of Thomas and Margrit was born 29 August 1730

Sarah HOVINGTON daughter of Thomas and Margrit born 20 November 1735

James COLLINS married Mary LANKFORD 14 July 1723

Mary COLLINS daughter of James and Mary was born 23 June 1726

Henry Smith ADAMS son of Rev. Alexander and Sarah was born 26 Mar.1739

Ezekiell TALOR son of Abraham and Rebeccah was born 15 October 1738

George BENNIT married Jane LINCH 13 December 1733

Jane BENNIT daughter of George and Jane was born 5 November 1737

Betty TULLEY daughter of James and Susanah was born 10 May 1739

Douty COLLIER married Pricilah NICHOLS 9 April 1737

Mary COLLIER daughter of Douty and Pricilah was born 7 June 1738

James NICHOLS married Phillis HARDY 10 January 1723

Isbell NICHOLS daughter of James and Phillis was born 22 October 1724

Joshua NICHOLS son of James and Phillis was born 3 August 1726

James NICHOLS son of James and Phillis was born 15 April 1728

John NICHOLS son of James and Phillis was born 22 July 1731

Charles NICHOLS son of James and Phillis was born 26 January 1732

Rachell NICHOLS daughter of James and Phillis was born 21 July 1736

Mary NICHOLS daughter of James and Phillis was born 15 February 1738

Thomas BARKLEY married Margrit BLAYLOCK 17 June 1709

Sarah BARKLEY daughter of Thomas and Margrit was born 14 December 1724

John HOPKINS son of John married Elizabeth NICHOLS, widow 20 Aug.1736

George Collier HOPKINS son of John & Eliz. was born 5 March 1737

Kesiah RICHARDSON daughter of John and Rachel was born 28 April 1734

Pricey COOPER daughter of John and Alice was born 29 December 1737

Jacob MESICK married Ann WILLING 28 October 1734

Betty MESICK daughter of Jacob and Ann was born 27 May 1736

Nehemiah MESICK son of Jacob and Ann was born 27 September 1738

Thomas JACKSON married Sarah HUMPHRIES 7 October 1735

Mary JACKSON daughter of Thomas and Sarah was born 22 June 1736

Betty JACKSON daughter of Thomas and Sarah was born 20 June 1738

Daniel WALTER married Sarah SAMUELS 25 January 1730

John WALTER son of Daniel and Sarah was born 25 September 1732

Ann WALTER daughter of Daniel and Sarah was born 11 May 1734

Samuel WALTER son of Daniel and Sarah was born 9 March 1736

George WALTER son of Daniel and Sarah was born 14 May 1738

Betty DUN daughter of Richard and Alice was born 11 July 1729

Sarah DUN daughter of Richard and Alice was born 16 September 1733

Richard DUN son of Richard and Alice was born 15 march 1737

Ann JONES daughter of Thomas and Susanah was born 28 May 1739

John FLEWELLING son of Samuel and Jane was born 17 February 1738/9

Martha BLUETT daughter of John and Marion was born 6 September 1739

John BUCKLEY married Elizabeth ANDERSON 26 January 1727

Betty BUCKLEY daughter of Nicholas and Eliz. was born 25 October 1731

William BUCKLEY son of Nicholas and ELizabeth was born 29 April 1733

Sarah BUCKLEY daughter of Nicholas and Eliz. was born 3 April 1735

Joseph BUCKLEY son of Nicholas and Elizbeth was born 19 April 1737

Thomas STEVANS son of William and Mary was born 28 August 1734

William STEVANS son of William and Mary was born 28 February 1726/7

Joseph HUSK married Mary STEVANS 7 February 1728

James HUSK son of Joseph and Mary was born 10 October 1730

Joseph HUSK son of Joseph and Mary was born 10 March 1731/2

John HUSK son of Joseph and Mary was born 20 April 1735

Archeybald HUSK son of Joseph and Mary was born 9 January 1737/8

John WILLEN son of Edward and Hanah was born 5 April 1730

Evains WILLIN son of Edward and Hannah was born 22 October 1732

Charles WILLIN son of Edward and Hannah was born 19 January 1734

William WILLIN son of Edward and Hannah was born 14 May 1738

George PHILLIPS son of Richard Jr. and Ann was born 15 July 1738

William GILES son of Thomas and Ann was born 13 March 1739

Cannon WINRIGHT son of Cannon and Rebecah was born 18 November 1733

Stevan WINRIGHT son of Cannon and Rebecah was born 9 May 1736

Solomon WINRIGHT son of Cannon and Rebeccah was born 9 June 1739/40

Aron READY son of Brion and Katherine was born 14 March 1738/9

Stevan WINRIGHT married Mary EVAINS 13 August 1737

Sarah WINRIGHT daughter of Stevan and Mary was born 20 December 1737

Betty DASHIELL wife of Col. George died 15 November 1739

William WINDER son of John and Jane was born 16 March 1714/5

Evains WINRIGHT son of Stevan and Mary was born 1 November 1739

Sarah COLLINS daughter of James and Mary was born 18 January 1728

Ann COLLINS daughter of James and Mary was born 29 February 1730

James COLLINS son of James and Mary was born in 1732

Honnour COLLINS daughter of James and Mary was born in 1735

John WILLIAMS married Rachell MOORE 12 September 1731

Edmund WILLIAMS son of John and Rachell was born 17 June 1832

Elizabeth WILLIAMS daughter of John and Rachell was born 14 Feb.1733/4

Josehua WILLIAMS son of John and Rachell was born 21 November 1736

Robert ATKINS married Elizabeth HIGHWAY 10 June 1711

Alice ATKINS daughter of Robert and Elizabeth was born 29 October 1714

Mary ATKINS daughter of Robert and Elizabeth was born 16 May 1717

Elizabeth ATKINS daughter of Robert Atkins and Eliza. born 10 Dec.1719

Hester ATKINS daughter of Robert and Eliza. was born 2 September 1722

William ATKINS son of Robert and Elizabeth was born 29 July 1725

Thomas ATKINS son of Robert and Elizabeth was born 4 January 1729

Leonard MARTIN son of John and Mary was born 14 November 1729

Matthew DUNKIN son of James and Catherine was born 10 August 1729

Jamima DUNKIN daughter of James and Katherine was born 2 November 1731

Margrit DUNKIN daughter of James and Katherine born 25 February 1733/4

James DUNKIN son of James and Katherine was born 6 February 1736/7

John Huett NUTTER married Margrit CARLILE 13 August 1727

John Huett NUTTER son of John and Margit was born 3 April 1730

Charles NUTTER son of John H. and Margrit was born 1 January 1732/3

Margrit NUTTER wife of John Huett died 27 January 1733/4

John Huett NUTTER married Ann NUTTER 4 April 1735

Ann NUTTER daughter of John H. and Ann was born 8 April 1736

Matthew NUTTER son of John H. and Ann was born 25 November 1737

Ester COTTMAN daughter of Joseph and Hannah was born 25 April 1739

Alexander LACKEY married Ann NUTTER, widow of Matthew 24 April 1724

John LACKEY son of Alexander and Ann died 1 October 1738

Ann COLLIER daughter of Douty and Pricilah was born 25 January 1739/40

Mary ATKINS daughter of Robert and Elizabeth was born 19 May 1717

Charles VAUGHN son of William and Mary was born 24 January 1739/40

George BACON son of Dudson and Elizabeth was born 20 July 1739

Elizabeth RODES daughter of John & Sarah was born 20 February 1739/40

Alexander Thomas RUSSELL married Ann PRICE 2 September 1740

John JONES son of John and Margrit was born 1 November 1739

Nanney Day SCOTT daughter of Day and Alice was born 6 June 1739

Sarah BOUNDS daughter of Joseph and Tabitha was born 13 August 1738

Elinor CORDRY daughter of Daniel and Rachel was born 17 Jan. 1737/8

Capt. Clement DASHIELL married Sarah PIPER daughter of William 1
January 1740/1

Mary DASHIELL daughter of Robert and Easter born 2 November 1740

Richard WALTER married Ann COTTMAN 28 August 1740

John DISHROON son of John Jr. and Francis born 14 March 1739/40

John SHILES Jr. married Ann EVAINS 14 September 1737

John SHILES son of John and Ann was born 9 September 1739

Ann & Edward MEGLAMRY son and daughter of Edward and Ann were born 3
February 1739/40

Mary PHILLIPS daughter of Richard and Ann was born 16 October 1740

George BENNIT son of George and Jane was born 15 January 1740/1

Jacob WOOTEN son of John and Margrit was born 3 July 1739

Mary WOOTEN daughter of John and Margrit was born 8 December 1740/1

Mary BENNIT daughter of Edward and Sarah was born 8 July 1741

Jessey BOUNDS son of Joseph and Tabitha was born 22 November 1740

Thomas RICHARDS married Sarah LAMEE 20 April 1740

Esther RICHARDS daughter of Thomas and Sarah was born 1 March 1741/2

William RICHARDS son of Alexander and Catherine born 16 March 1740

Elizabeth RITCHIE daughter of Archibald and Eliz. born 3 October 1741/2 and died 5 April 1742

Pricilah DASHIELL daughter in law of Joseph died 7 March 1742

Bridget COLLIER daughter of Douty and Pricillah born 26 September 1742

William GILES second married Sarah PIPER 10 August 1741

Mary GILES daughter of William Jr.and Sarah was born 23 October 1742

Rachell RUSSELL daughter of Alexander Thomas and Ann born 27 June 1741

Nanney BOUNDS daughter of Joseph and Tabitha was born 21 March 1742/3

John JONES son of Thomas and Susanah was born 16 January 1741 and died 26 September 1742

John FLEWELLING son of Samuel and Jane was born 17 February 1738/9

George DASHIELL son of George and Eliz. was born 28 August 1743

Mary MORRISS daughter of Joseph and Mary was born 26 June 1743

Thomas ROBERSON son of William and Sarah was born August 1725

James HARDY married Winefred CORNISH 24 February 1739/40

Elizabeth WALTER daughter of John and Easter was born 25 April 1744

John HARRIS son of William and Mary was born 12 August 1739

Thomas HARRIS son of William and Mary was born 22 January 1741

Samuel FLEWELLING son of Samuel and Jane was born 11 August 1744

James STUART son of Dr. Patrick and Emme was born 10 October 1744

Emme STEWART wife of Dr. Patrick died 17 December 1744

Nanney Day SCOTT daughter of Day and Alice was born 25 June 1739

George SCOTT died 3 November 1741, age 64 or 65.

Sarah Day SCOTT daughter of Day and Alice was born 6 November 1742

Joshua BENNIT son of Edward and Sarah was born 6 September 1743

Solomon SMITH son of Andrew Jr. and Sarah was born 10 March 1742

Dennis DULANY married Judah ODONOHO 1734

Daniel DULANY son of Dennis and Judah was born 7 August 1737

Mary DULANEY daughter of Dennis and Judah was born 15 November 1739

Paule DULANEY son of Dennis and Judah was born 12 November 1741

Elizabeth DULANEY daughter of Dennis and Judah was born 23 July 1744

James RICHARDS Jr. son of Thomas and Sarah was born 10 July 1744 and
died.

Thomas RICORDS Jr. son of Thomas and Sarah was born 10 October 1745

Elizabeth RICORDS daughter of Alexander and Katherine born 1 May 1743

Alexander ADAMS Jr. married Sarah JONES 19 May 1745

Ann GILES daughter of Thomas and Ann was born 8 February 1742

John GILES son of Thomas and Ann was born 27 April 1746

Kesiah BOUNDS daughter of Joseph and Tabitha was born 8 February 1745

Esther DASHIELL daughter of Robert and Esther was born 6 December 1742

Robert DASHIELL Died 20 August 1744

Rachell LARRIMORE daughter of James and Eliz. born 11 November 1744

Edward Day SCOTT son of Day and Alice was born 17 March 1744

Mrs. Alice SCOTT died 20 March 1744, age 32 in childbirth.

Day SCOTT son of Day and Esther was born 13 December 1746

Levin WINRIGHT son of Cannon and Rebecca was born 31 October 1742

John WINRIGHT son of Cannon and Rebecca was born 1 May 1744

Elizabeth EDGE daughter of Joshua and Eliza was born 8 November 1741

Obediah EDGE son of Joshua and Eliza was born 19 February 1745

James JONES son of Thomas and Susanah was born 5 April 1746

John AERSKIN son of Samuel and Judah was born 21 July 1746

John RICHARDSON married Mary WALKER 21 November 1742

Mary RICHARDSON daughter of John and Mary was born 29 october 1743

Elizabeth RICHARDSON daughter of John and Mary was born 13 July 1746

Thomas WALKER died 29 December 1744

Richard TULLEY married Mary TALOR 23 May 1745

Mary TULLEY daughter of Richard and Mary was born 11 March 17456

Katherine TULLEY daughter of Richard and Mary born 19 January 1747/8

John KILLAMS married Sarah McCLESTER 24 November 1738

Daniel KILLAMS son of John and Sarah was born 23 January 1742

Isabell KILLAMS daughter of John and Sarah was born 23 October 1744

Edward KILLIAMS son oof John and Sarah was born 21 September 1746

John EVAINS JR. married Mary EVAINS 7 March 1738/9

Sarah EVAINS daughter of John and Mary was born 23 January 1740/1

John EVAINS son of John and Mary was born 4 May 1744

Nicholas EVAINS son of John and Mary was born 7 September 1746

Phillis TALOR daughter of William and Sarah was born 11 November 1742

Elizabeth WALTER daughter of Thomas Jr. and Jane born 20 April 1740

Mary WALTER daughter of Thomas and Jane was born 26 September 1742

Thomas WALTER son of Thomas and Jane was born 13 February 1744/5

Pricalah WALTER daughter of Thomas and Jane was born 22 July 1747

James ENGLISH married Ame WALTER 10 February 1743/4

Mary ENGLISH daughter of James and Amey was born 10 August 1745

Eliner ENGLISH daughter of James and Amey was born 24 February 1747/8

William WALTER married Rachel JONES 18 August 1744

James WALTER son of William and Rachel was born 18 June 1745

Sarah WALTER daughter of William and Rachel was born 10 June 1748

Betty DAVIS daughter of William and Bridget was born 7 September 1730

Joseph ALLEN married BETTY DAVIS 9 September 1748

William Davis ALLEN son of Joseph and Betty was born 21 August 1749

John Day SCOTT son of Day and Esther was born 15 October 1748

Esther SCOTT wife of Day died 17 December 1748, age 29.

George BENNIT son of George and Jane was born 22 March 1749/50

Stevan BENNIT son of Edward and Sarah was born 2 June 1746

William KINNINGHAM son of Thomas and Sarah was born 29 May 1735

Thomas KINNINGHAM son of Thomas and Sarah was born 24 December 1737

Patrick STUART married Emme CHAPMAN in London 17 November 1725

Gilbert STUART son of Patrick and Emme born 12 September 1726

Ann STUART daughter of Patrick and Emme was born 14 April 1736

Isabel STUART daughter of Patrick and Emme was born 2 May 1737

Robert STUART son of Patrick and Emmie was born 24 June 1738

Elizabeth STUART daughter of Patrick and Emmie was born 28 May 1740

William STUART son of Patrick and Emmie was born 28 January 1741/2

Thomas MOOR son of William married Ann STEVANS widow, 7 July 1751

Louther DASHIELL married Anna PIPER daughter of William 19 Nov.1743

Jane DASHIELL daughter of Luther and Anna was born 26 July 1745

Milcah DASHIELL daughter of Luther and Anna was born 20 January 1746/7

Nicholas Evans COLLIER married Ann COLLIER 5 March 1746/7

Jane COLLIER daughter of Nicholas Evans and Ann born 20 August 1747

George COLLIER son of Nicholas Evans and Ann born 23 December 1750

John HARDY married Ann NUTTER 25 December 1748

Thomas HARDY son of John and Ann was born 18 March 1749/50

Nicholas EVANS married Priscilla GILLIS 27 July 1749

John EVANS son of Nicholas and Priscilla was born 23 June 1750

Sarah KILLAM daughter of John and Sarah was born 11 June 1751

Thomas GILES married Ann HARRIS 12 March 1750

Sarah GILES daughter of Thomas and Ann was born 19 April 1752

Charity BENNIT daughter of George and Jane was born 8 April 1752

Mary DASHIELL daughter of Capt.Clement and Sarah born 24 December 1741

Sarah DASHIELL daughter of Capt. Clement and Sarah born 27 July 1744

Josiah DASHIELL son of Capt.Clement and Sarah was born 12 October 1746

Clement DASHIELL son of Capt. Clement and Sarah born 9 December 1748

Nancey DASHIELL daughter of Capt.Clement and Sarah born 9 October 1751

Thomas TODVINE married Mary BALY 6 October 1745

Ellinor TODVINE daughter of Thomas and Mary was born 30 August 1746

Henry TODVINE son of Thomas and Mary was born 11 July 1748

Thomas TODVINE son of Thomas and Mary was born 5 November 1750

Stevan TODVINE son of Thomas and Mary was born 18 January 1753

Joseph WAILES son of Daniel and Betty was born 15 September 1753

Steven HAITH son of Abraham and Pricila was born 1 August 1746

Matthew HAITH son of Abraham and Pricila was born 4 March 1748

Elinor HAITH daughter of Abraham and Pricila born 8 February 1749/50

Sarah HAITH daughter of Abraham and Pricila born 17 March 1751/2

Daniel GAME son of Dr. Henry and Rose was born 10 August 1751

Bridget GAME daughter of Henry and Rose was born 20 February 1754

William Gilberd GRAY son of William and Sarah was born 22 May 1739

Sarah Foskey GRAY daughter of Wm. and Sarah was born 30 August 1741

Joseph Foskey GRAY son of Wm. and Sarah (twin)was born 30 August 1741

William GRAY married Patience ELLINGSWORTH,widow, 28 May 1743

Andrew Francis CHENEY (Chirgeon)son of James of Mt. Cherrey County
Cork Ireland married Mary Day SCOTT daughter of Day 15 July 1755

Levin HOPKINS son of Isaac and Margrit was born 31 December 1748

Jane HOPKINS daughter of Isaac and Margrit was born 8 March 1750

William Nicholason HOPKINS son of Isaac and Margrit born 4 April 1752

George HOPKINS son of Isaac and Margrit was born 31 October 1754

John BEARD son of James and Sarah was born 23 April 1750

James BEARD son of James and Sarah was born 14 March 1752

Thomas BEARD son of James and Sarah was born 6 November 1755

James CHENEY son of Andrew Francis and Mary born 5 May 1756 and was Christened by Rev. Alexander ADAMS, Rector of Stepney parish, his godfather. Major Day SCOTT, Tubman LOWS, and godmother Mis. Ann Day SCOTT.

Jacob MORRIS son of Joseph and Ann was born 1 July 1746

Joseph MORRIS son of Joseph and Ann was born 1 February 1747/8

William DISHEROON married Mary PULLETT 22 September 1736

Priscilla DISHEROON daughter of Wm. and Mary was born 13 May 1743

Jesse DISHEROON son of William and Mary was born 18 April 1745

Elijah DISHEROON son of William and Mary was born 8 November 1746

Levin DISHEROON son of William and Mary was born 24 December 1741

Margaret DISHEROON daughter of William and Mary born 18 August 1737

Waitman DISHEROON son of William and Mary was born 21 September 1748

Joshua DISHEROON son of William and Mary was born 2 January 1749

Jarvis JENKINS married Sarah KIBBLE 29 January 1744/45

Mary JENKINS daughter of Jarvis and Sarah was born 5 September 1746

Anne JENKINS daughter of Jarvis and Sarah was born 4 January 1748/9

Sarah JENKINS daughter of Jarvis and Sarah was born 1 September 1750

Hannah JENKINS daughter of Jarvis and Sarah was born 13 April 1753

Kibble JENKINS son of Jarvis and Sarah was born 8 February 1756

Alexander ROBERTSON married Leah DENNIS 3 February 1755

James ROBERTSON son of Alexander and Leah was born 19 January 1756

Joseph MORRIS married Elizabeth MALLONE 14 December 1756

Isaac COLLINS son of Thomas and Rebeka was born 14 May 1753

Moses LINDOW son of Rebecka born at Arnold ELZEY's 18 December 1753

Thomas DASHIELL married Ann GUIBERT 8 May 1757

Levin WILLSON son of George and Phiriba was born 11 February 1757

Capt. Joseph DASHIELL married Martha BLUETT 18 May 1757

Stephen MAGEE son of Peter and Elizabeth was born 29 July 1755

Thomas HOLEBROOK married Sarah HAMILTON ,widow 21 August 1756

Thomas HOLEBROOK son of Thomas and Sarah was born 7 July 1757

Anne EVANS daughter of Nicholas and Prsicilla was born 27 July 1752

Thomas EVANS son of Nicholas and Priscilla was born 12 March 1755

Prisee EVANS daughter of Nicholas and Priscilla born 3 August 1757

Samuel RADISH son of HIERON and Elizabeth was born 28 September 1756

John CROUCH married Elizabeth EVANS 24 February 1744/5

Robert CROUCH son of John and Elizabeth was born 7 November 1746

Ezekiel CROUCH son of John and Elizabeth was born 8 March 1749

Elizabeth CROUCH daughter of John and Elizabeth born 13 April 1751

Ely CROUCH son of John and Elizabeth was born 4 April 1755

John MORRIS married Mary SHERMAN 1 October 1744

Samuel MORRIS son of John and Mary was born 27 July 1746

John MORRIS son of John and Mary was born 21 July 1748

Elizabeth MORRIS daughter of John and Mary was born 5 May 1750

Jonathan MORRIS son of John and Mary was born 27 March 1752

Mary MORRIS daughter of John and Mary was born 28 July 1754

Joshua MORRIS son of John and Mary was born 18 January 1757

Joseph MORRIS married Mary STEVENS 13 November 1730

George WILSON son of George and Phiribey was born 13 September 1758

James ROBERTSON son of Alexander and Leah was born 28 October 1758

John CHRISTOPHER married Sarah STANFORD 26 February 1759

Hugh KENNEDY married Sarah RADISH 25 July 1745

Elizabeth KENNEDY daughter of Hugh and Sarah was born 13 July 1746

John RADISH KENNEDY son of Hugh and Sarah was born 12 September 1748

Sarah KENNEDY daughter of Hugh and Sarah was born 12 February 1751

William KENNEDY son of Hugh and Sarah was born 27 July 1753

George KENNEDY son of Hugh and Sarah was born 8 October 1757

Andrew ADAMS married Mary WHITTINGHAM 25 February 1759

Jesse DASHIELL married Susanna TOWNSEND 10 August 1739

James DASHIELL son of Jesse and Susanna was born 13 August 1740

Sarah DASHIELL daughter of Jesse and Susanna was born 16 April 1744

Benjamin DASHIELL son of Jesse and Susanna was born 3 March 1745

Susanna DASHIELL daughter of Jesse and Susanna born 27 February 1747

Jesse DASHIELL son of Jesse and Susanna was born 3 June 1752

John DASHIELL son of Jesse and Susanna was born 11 August 1757

William HITCH married Ann COLLINS 22 October 1755

Sophia HITCH daughter of William and Ann was born 31 July 1756

Mary RECORDS daughter of Thomas and Sarah was born 1 November 1748

Ann RECORDS daughter of Thomas and Sarah was born March 1752

Sarah Lamee RECORDS daughter of Thomas and Sarah born 14 April 1755

Euphrosina RECORDS daughter of Thomas and Sarah born 24 December 1757

Thomas HUMPHRISS married Temperance MORRISS 23 April 1736

Jemima HUMPHRISS daughter of Thomas and Temperance born 5 July 1738

Thomas HUMPHRISS son of Thomas and Temperance born 19 November 1739

John HUMPHRISS son Thomas and Temperance was born 13 April 1741

Jacob HUMPHRISS son of Thomas and Temperance was born 1 March 1743

Joseph HUMPHRISS son of Thomas and Temperance was born 14 January 1745

Mary HUMPHRISS daughter of Thomas and Temperance born 13 January 1747

Rachel HUMPHRISS daughter of Thomas & Temperance born 3 February 1749

Thomas PRICE married Patience KIBBLE 22 December 1756

Patience KIBBLE daughter of John and Sarah born 25 September 1738

Nathaniel WALLER married Elizabeth STROBRIDGE 21 September 1741

Zephaniah WALLER son of Nathaniel and Elizabeth born 28 February 1744

Nathaniel WALLER son of Nathaniel and Elizabeth born 9 September 1746

John WALLER son of Nathaniel and Elizabeth was born 13 March 1749

Joseph WALLER son of Nathaniel and Elizabeth was born 22 November 1751

Nelly WALLER daughter of Nathaniel & Eliz. was born 12 September 1754

Elisabeth WALLER daughter of Nathaniel & Eliz. was born 23 May 1757

Hannah STEVENS daughter of John and Anne was born 25 February 1721

William KIBBLE married Hannah STEVENS 20 April 1736

William KIBBLE son of William and Hannah was born 21 September 1740

George KIBBLE son of William and Hannah was born 17 January 1744

Anne Stevens KIBBLE daughter of Wm. and Hannah born 1 January 1746/7

John DEVEREAUX son of John and Anne was born 4 October 1740

Ephraim KING Married Anne HANDY, widow, 6 March 1757

Samuel KING son of Ephraim and Anne was born 25 October 1758

Henry DASHIELL maried Sarah RENSHAW 1 January 1755

Levi DASHIELL son of Henry and Sarah was born 2 May 1757

John PARRAMORE married Ellinor WALLER 28 August 1743

Thomas PARRAMORE son of John and Ellinor was born 26 May 1745

John PARRAMORE son of John and Ellinor was born 9 November 1751

Betty PARRAMORE daughter of John and Ellinor was born 14 June 1753

Nathaniel PARRAMORE son of John and Ellinor was born 13 March 1756

Ellinor PARRAMORE daughter of John and Ellinor born 24 December 1758

Robert HITCH married Eve HITCH 14 February 1751

Isaac HITCH son of Robert and Eve was born 13 December 1754

Phillis HITCH daughter of Robert and Eve was born 5 November 1756

Delilah HITCH daughter of Robert and Eve was born 4 June 1759

Ebenezer WALLER son of Richard and Ann was born 8 January 1742

William Cottman WALLER son of Richard and Ann born 14 October 1743

Mary WALLER daughter of Richard and Ann was born 22 March 1745

Richard WALLER son of Richard and Ann was born 4 May 1747

Thomas WALLER son of Richard and Ann was born 28 January 1749

George WALLER son of Richard and Ann was born 1 October 1750

Jonathan WALLER son of Richard and Ann was born 1 September 1752

Ann WALLER daughter of Richad and Ann was born 29 October 1754

Job SHERMAN married Abigail KIBBLE 5 February 1733

Ellinor SHERMAN daughter of Job and Abigail was born 17 November 1735

Louther SHERMAN son of Job and Abigail was born 1 January 1737

Temperance SHERMAN on of Job and Abigail was born 9 August 1739

Patience SHERMAN daughter of Job and Abigail was born 3 April 1742

William SHERMAN son of Job and Abigail was born 24 March 1745

Abigail SHERMAN daughter of Job and Abigail was born 22 December 1747

Job SHERMAN son of Job and Abigail was born 6 May 1749

Comfort PECK of Providence, Rhode Island married Priscilla GREEN 11 December 1750.

Martha Bluet DASHIELL daughter of Joseph and Martha born 7 April 1759

Thomas DASHIELL married Jane RENSHAW 29 October 1747

Alice DASHIELL daughter of Thomas and Jane was born 13 May 1749

Sarah DASHIELL daughter of Thomas and Jane was born 2 June 1751

Matthias DASHIELL son of Thomas and Jane was born 16 September 1753

Ann DASHIELL daughter of Thomas and Jane was born 28 March 1756

Mary DASHIELL daughter of Thomas and Jane was born 2 March 1759

Betty MOOR daughter of Thomas and Ann was born 23 March 1755

William MOOR son of Thomas and Ann was born 18 April 1757

Ephraim MOOR son of Thomas and Ann was born 16 November 1759

Jane DASHIELL daughter of Thomas and Jane was born 13 May 1761

John ADAMS married Sarah DASHIELL, widow, 15 February 1760

Isaac HOPKINS married Margaret NICHOLSON 18 April 1747

Mary HOPKINS daughter of Isaac and Margaret was born 11 May 1757

William ROBERTSON married Sarah DASHIELL 1 May 1743

Joseph ROBERTSON son of William and Sarah was born 22 October 1755

William ROBERTSON son of William and Sarah was born 5 September 1757

Peggy ROBERTSON daughter of Wm. and Sarah was born 13 March 1760

Stephen LANGCAKE married Betty HARRIS 27 January 1745

William LANGCAKE son of Stephen and Betty was born 27 September 1748

Cannon LANGCAKE son of Stephen and Betty was born 5 November 1750

George LANGCAKE son of Stephen and Betty was born 14 February 1752

Nehemiah LANGCAKE son of Stephen and Betty was born 3 December 1754

Frances LANGCAKE daughter of Stephen and Betty born 15 October 1756

Esther PRICE daughter of Thomas and Patience was born 1 August 1760

Charity BENNIT daughter of George and Jane was born 17 April 1752

Isaac SHERMAN married Sarah LINCH 28 May 1740

Mary SHERMAN daughter of Isaac and Sarah was born 18 July 1747

Sarah SHERMAN daughter of Isaac and Sarah was born 27 September 1751

Leah SHERMAN daughter of Isaac and Sarah was born 1 January 1754

Betty SHERMAN daughter of Isaac and Sarah was born 19 June 1758

Joseph VENABLES married Nelly POLK 8 June 1756

Betty VENABLES daughter of Joseph and Nelly was born 29 May 1757

Benjamin VENABLES son of Joseph and Nelly was born 1 December 1758

George WAILES married Betty TAYLOR 25 August 1754

Eleanor WAILES daughter of George and Betty was born 16 June 1755

Mary WAILES daughter of George and Betty was born 22 November 1757

Levin WAILES son of George and Betty was born 3 May 1760

Thomas ENGLISH son of James and Amay was born 3 December 1750

James ENGLISH son of James and Amay was born 12 July 1753

William ENGLISH son of James and Amay was born 1 February 1755

Levin ENGLISH son of James and Amay was born 14 April 1759

Charles RECORDS son of Alexander and Katherine born 2 February 1746

Kathrine RECORDS daughter of Alexander and Katherine born 1 Dec. 1748

Sarah RECORDS daughter of Alexander and Katherine born 12 Sept. 1752

Eleanor RECORDS daughter of Alexander and Katherine born 9 June 1755

Alexander RECORDS son of Alexander and Katherine born 4 Sep.1758

William BENNIT married Dorithy PULLY 13 May 1754

Anna BENNIT daughter of Wm. and Dorithy was born 27 June 1756

William BENNIT son of William and Dorithy was born 11 September 1758

John BENNIT son of William and Dorithy was born 29 September 1760

Nice WALLER daughter of William and Rachel was born 13 April 1751

Rachel WALLER daughter of William and Rachel was born 24 March 1754

William WALLER son of William and Rachel was born 12 February 1757

Ephraim WALLER son of William and Rachel was born 19 January 1760

Thomas COLLINS married Rebecka STEVENS 28 December 1741

Elizabeth COLLINS daughter of Thomas and Rebecka born 26 August 1744

Anne COLLINS daughter of Thomas and Rebecka was born 15 March 1747

Mary COLLINS daughter of Thomas and Rebecka was born 2 December 1749

Isaac COLLINS son of Thomas and Rebecka was born 14 May 1753

Rebecka COLLINS daughter of Thomas and Rebecka was born 29 June 1755

Thomas COLLINS son of Thomas and Rebecka was born 12 June 1760

George Day SCOTT married Elisabeth HANDY 21 March 1760

John ANDERSON married Sarah SHERMAN 22 September 1749

John ANDERSON son of John and Sarah was born 14 February 1752

George ANDERSON son of John and Sarah was born 20 June 1755

Richard Stephens BOUNDS married Mary STEVENS 10 August 1752

James BOUNDS son of Richard and Mary was born 19 April 1753

Jonathan BOUNDS son of Richard and Mary was born 8 May 1757

Richard Stevens BOUNDS son of Richard S. & Mary was born 10 June 1759

Mattilda RICHARDSON daughter of John and Mary born 24 March 1749/50

Mary STEVENS daughter of John and Anne was born 24 December 1719

James RAEY of Arman in the County of Arundale in Scotland, married Ellinor STEVENS 11 June 1761.

Isaac DASHIELL married Henrietta SCARBURGH 13 August 1747

Alice DASHIELL daughter of Isaac and Henrietta born 13 October 1748

Betty DASHIELL daughter of Isaac and Henrietta born 17 November 1752

Isaac DASHIELL son of Isaac and Henrietta was born 5 April 1757

Henry DASHIELL son of Isaac and Henrietta was born 5 October 1759

Rachell HITCH daughter of Robert and Eve was born 17 November 1760

Nicholas Evans COLLIER married Rebecka EVANS 6 March 1758

Nicholas Evans COLLIER son of Nicholas and Rebecka born 31 August 1758

Elisabeth COLLIER daughter of Nicholas & Rebecka born 18 December 1759

Priscilla COLLIER daughter of Nicholas and Ann was born 9 April 1753

Nicholas COLLIER son of Nicholas E. and Ann was born 5 October 1755

James BOUNDS son of Richard Stevens and Mary was born 1 October 1762

John ADAMS married Sarah DASHIELL, widow 14 February 1760

John ADAMS son of John and Sarah was born 21 November 1760

William ADAMS son of John and Sarah was born 19 February 1765

Jesse HUGHES son of Hezekiah and Mary was born 28 February 1768

Jesse HUGHES married Sarah McCLISTER 4 October 1789

Sarah JONES daughter of Benjamin and Betty was born 3 June 1759

Arthur DASHIELL son of Louther and Anna was born 2 July 1752

William DASHIELL son of Louther and Anna was born 26 September 1754

George DASHIELL son of Louther DASHIELL and Anna born 18 March 1759

Matthias DASHIELL son of Louther and Anna was born 11 April 1761

George DASHIELL married Arasy FISHER 6 August 1760

James Fairfax DASHIELL son of George and Arasy was born 5 May 1761

Richard BIGLANDS of Whitehaven in the County of Cumberland England
married Mary KIBBLE 22 March 1749

Margaret BIGLANDS daughter of Richard and Mary born 26 February 1750

Mary BIGLANDS daughter of Richard and Mary born 15 February 1753

Anne BIGLANDS daughter of Richard and Mary was born 16 February 1754

John BIGLANDS son of Richard and Mary was born 21 February 1756

William BIGLANDS son of Richard and Mary was born 19 August 1758

Clement CHRISTOPHER son of Clement and Sarah was born 9 January 1740

Newell CHRISTOPHER daughter of Clement & Sarah was born 22 July 1742

Sarah CHRISTOPHER daughter of Clement and Sarah was born 14 June 1744

Edward CHRISTOPHER son of Clement and Sarah was born 21 July 1746

Elijah CHRISTOPHER son of Clement and Sarah was born 16 July 1750

Anne CHRISTOPHER daughter of Clement and Sarah born 25 February 1755

James STEWART son of Patrick and Emme was born 21 October 1744

John GOSLEE married Hannah TULL 10 September 1754

Betty GOSLEE daughter of John and Hannah was born 13 July 1755

Matthew GOSLEE son of John and Hannah was born 3 December 1757

Rachel GOSLEE daughter of John and Hannah was born 22 January 1761

Thomas RUSSEL son of Thomas and Mary was born 2 March 1740/1

George SHARP married Hannah BAILY 25 February 1759

Eleanor SHARP daughter of George and Hannah was born 3 November 1759

Mary Lockerman ALLEN daughter of Joseph and Betty born 13 January 1754

Edward BENNITT married Priscilla COVENTON 13 October 1756
James BENNITT son of Edward and Priscilla born 28 December 1757

31

Jane Coventon BENNITT daughter of Edward & Priscilla born 23 Dec.1759

Daniel GOSLEE married Elizabeth TULLY, widow 2 July 1747

Thomas GOSLEE son of Daniel and Elizabeth was born 23 September 1749

Joshua GOSLEE son of Daniel and Elizabeth was born 24 April 1751

George GOSLEE son of Daniel and Elizabeth was born 13 January 1753

Betty GOSLEE daughter of Daniel and Elizabeth was born 21 August 1757

Daniel SHARP son of George and Hannah was born 27 April 1762

Benjamin MORRIS son of Joseph and Elisabeth was born 1 May 1759

John Mallone MORRIS son of Joseph and ELisabeth born 18 November 1761

William COLLINS son of Thomas and Rebecca was born 19 July 1762

John WALLER married Mary HOFFINGTON 18 August 1751

Jonathan WALLER son of John and Mary was born 18 August 1752

Betty WALLER daughter of John and Mary was born 19 May 1756

Sarah WALLER daughter of John and Mary was born 9 October 1758

Littleton WALLER son of John and Mary was born 31 March 1761

Aaron CARTER married Mary WALLER 13 December 1751

James CARTER son of Aaron and Mary was born 26 May 1752

Joseph CARTER son of Aaron and Mary was born 31 January 1754

Jane CARTER daughter of Aaron and Mary was born 12 March 1756

Priscilla ENGLISH daughter of James and Mary was born 8 February 1762

Archelaus RECORDS son of Thomas and Sarah was born 2 July 1760

Arnold TODVINE son of Thomas and Mary was born 29 January 1755

Mary TODVINE daughter of Thomas and Mary was born 6 October 1762

Robert MACCELPIN married Jane JOHNSON 4 December 1732

Craford MACCEPLIN son of Robert and Jane was born 14 May 1738

John HOLBROOK son of Thomas and Sarah was born 9 August 1759

Henry HOLBROOK son of Thomas and Sarah was born 1 November 1761

Thomas FLETCHER married Elisabeth MOOR 23 June 1757

Sarah FLETCHER daughter of Thomas and Elisabeth was born 15 May 1758

Nancey FLETCHER daughter of Thomas and Elisabeth born 11 June 1759

Elisabeth FLETCHER daughter of Thomas & Elisabeth born 4 October 1760

Mary FLETCHER daughter of Thomas and Elisabeth was born 2 January 1763

George ROBERTSON son of Alexander and Leah was born 28 October 1760

John ROBERTSON son of Alexander and Leah was born 8 November 1762

John KIBBLE son of William and Hannah was born 6 April 1763

George GALE married Elizabeth AIREY 13 January 1750

Milcah GALE daughter of George and Elizabeth was born 20 June 1751

John GALE son of George and Elizabeth was born 25 September 1753

George GALE son of George and Elizabeth was born 9 May 1756

Mary GALE daughter of George and ELizabeth was born 14 April 1759

Mary GALE daughter of George and Elizabeth died 22 December 1760

Elizabeth GALE daughter of George and Elizabeth born 22 November 1762

George FLETCHER son of Rev. Thomas and Sarah was born 28 May 1741

Nathan COTMAN son of Sarah was born 14 January 1753/4

George LOE married Sarah COTMAN 29 December 1754

Phillis LOE daughter of George and Sarah was born 29 September 1755

Lidia LOE daughter of George and Sarah was born 8 August 1758

George LOE son of George and Sarah was born 8 July 1760

William LOE son of George and Sarah was born 28 November 1762

Lazarus HUFFINGTON married Mary HARRIS 23 November 1759

Sarah HUFFINGTON daughter of Lazarus and Mary born 23 September 1760

John GUPTON married Ann LANGFORD 17 April 1747

Elizabeth GUPTON daughter of John and Ann was born 3 August 1748

Ann GUPTON daughter of John and Ann was born 3 January 1753

Esther GUPTON daughter of John and Ann was born 8 June 1755

Jane GUPTON daughter of John and Ann was born 17 October 1758

Susannah GUPTON daughter of John and Ann was born 26 July 1760

William GUPTON son of John and Ann was born 1 March 1763

John NELLSON married Dinah MEZICK 13 January 1745

Susannah NELLSON daughter of John and Susannah was born 26 Feb.1746

James NELLSON son of John and Susannah was born 25 December 1747

Rebeka NELLSON daughter of John and Susannah born 22 April 1750

Benjamin NELLSON son of John and Susannah was born 29 July 1752

Sarah NELLSON daughter of John and Susannah was born 28 June 1755

John NELLSON son of John and Susannah was born 11 October 1758

Elizabeth NELLSON daughter of John and Susannah was born 11 Dec.1762

Levin MOOR married Mary DARBY 4 September 1757

William MOOR son of Levin and Mary was born 9 July 1758

Sarah MOOR daughter of Levin and Mary was born 14 March 1760

Levin MOOR son of Levin and Mary was born 16 August 1762

Josiah PHILLIPS married Elizabeth BENNET 23 November 1761

Priscilla Bennet PHILLIPS daughter of Josiah & ELiz. born 25 Oct.1762

William SHAW married Jane BENNET 18 March 1759

John SHAW son of William was born 20 December 1762

Benjamin VENABLES married Betty DASHIELL 9 June 1761

Nelly VENABLES daughter of Benjamin and Betty was born 2 May 1763

William PHILLIPS married Margaret LOW 22 January 1744

Eleanor PHILLIPS daughter of William and Margaret born 20 June 1744

Isaac PHILLIPS son of William and Margaret was born 13 February 1751

Elizabeth PHILLIPS daughter of Wm. and Margaret born 26 December 1753

Rachel PHILLIPS daughter of Wm. and Margaret born 10 October 1756

William PHILLIPS son of William and Margaret was born 20 January 1758

Elijah PHILLIPS son of William and Margaret was born 21 May 1760

Mary PHILLIPS daughter of William and Margaret born 25 November 1762

Thomas RALPH married Charity CALLAWAY 12 December 1751

Sarah RALPH daughter of Thomas and Charity was born 24 October 1752

Ephraim RALPH son of Thomas and Charity was born 11 November 1754

Esther RALPH daughter of Thomas and Charity was born 13 April 1757

Eunice RALPH daughter of Thomas and Charity was born 6 June 1759

Eleanor RALPH daughter of Thomas and Charity was born 29 October 1761

Richard PHILLIPS married Anne BENNET 4 January 1733/4

Daniel PHILLIPS son of Richard and Anne was born 27 October 1734

Betty PHILLIPS daughter of Richard and Anne was born 22 July 1736

George PHILLIPS son of Richard and Ann was born 15 July 1738

Mary PHILLIPS daughter of Richard and Anne was born 16 October 1740

Sarah PHILLIPS daughter of Richard and Anne was born 29 January 1742/3

Priscilla PHILLIPS daughter of Richard & Anne born 11 March 1744/5

Richard PHILLIPS son of Richard and Anne was born 16 February 1746/7

Joshua PHILLIPS son of Richard and Anne was born 2 December 1751

John FLETCHER married Rachel PARRAMORE,widow 3 April 1757

Mary FLETCHER daughter of John and Rachel was born 28 January 1757

Thomas FLETCHER son of John and Rachel was born 26 September 1759

Leah FLETCHER daughter of John and Rachel was born 17 May 1762

James ROBERTSON married Mary DEAN, widow 26 July 1746

Edward BENNETT son of William and Dorithy was born 27 February 1763

Edward BENNETT Jr. married Jane TULLY 10 March 1759

Littleton BENNETT son of Edward and Jane was born 21 October 1759

Richard HARRIS married Margaret GILES 24 September 1735

Mary HARRIS daughter of Richard and Margaret was born 13 January 1739

Levin HARRIS son of Richard and Margaret was born 18 April 1742

Eunice HARRIS daughter of Richard and Margaret was born 13 March 1747

John ROBERTSON married Priscilla WRIGHT 9 October 1755

Isaac ROBERTSON son of John and Priscilla was born 8 August 1756

William ROBERTSON son of John and Priscilla was born 1 November 1758

John ROBERTSON son of John and Priscilla was born 11 December 1760

Jacob ROBERTSON son of John and Priscilla was born 11 May 1763

James TAYLOR married Elizabeth ACKWORTH 22 August 1745

William TAYLOR son of James and Elizabeth was born 19 March 1748

Thomas TAYLOR son of James and Elizabeth was born 12 June 1750

John TAYLOR son of James and Elizabeth was born 19 May 1752

Joshua TAYLOR son of James and Elizabeth was born 23 March 1754

Benjamin TAYLOR son of James and Elizabeth was born 16 June 1756

John ELZEY married Major SHILES 19 May 1736

Mary ELZEY daughter of John and Major was born 26 March 1737/8

Arnold ELZEY son of John and Major was born 8 November 1740

Thomas ELZEY son of John and Major was born 23 September 1743

Nelly ELZEY daughter of John and Major was born 31 March 1746

John ELZEY married MARY COLLINS 20 February 1758

Major ELZEY daughter of John and Mary was born 18 January 1759

William ELZEY son of John and Mary was born 28 February 1761

Jacob WRIGHT married Betty BAILY 9 December 1756

Joshua WRIGHT son of Jacob and Betty was born 13 October 1757

Nelly WRIGHT daughter of Jacob and Betty was bon 12 November 1759

Isaac WRIGHT son of Jacob and Betty was born 25 May 1761

Levin WRIGHT was married to Elizabeth DARBY 24 September 1760

Esther WRIGHT daughter of Levin and Elizabeth born 11 December 1761

George PHILLIPS married Betty TWILLY, widow 11 Janury 1758

Ann PHILLIPS daughter of George and Betty was born 16 October 1758

George PHILLIPS son of George and Betty was born 23 June 1763

James TWILLEY married Mary PHILLIPS 6 April 1759

Betty TWILLEY daughter of James and Mary was born 21 February 1760

Ann TWILLEY daughter of James and Mary was born 4 June 1762

James WEST married Sarah HARRIS 3 February 1755

Mary WEST daughter of James and Sarah was born 11 January 1759

Sarah WEST daughter of James and Sarah was born 23 September 1761

Ralph LOW married Anne RENSHAW 15 September 1755

James LOW son of Ralph and Anne was born 26 June 1756

Eleanor LOW daughter of Ralph and Anne was born 16 April 1758

Ralph LOW son of Ralph and Anne was born 13 September 1762

Thomas ROBERTS married Elizabeth RENSHAW 28 October 1743

Fisher ROBERTS son of Thomas and Elizabeth was born 12 October 1744

Eleanor ROBERTS daughter of Thomas and Elizabeth born 2 February 1746

Sarah ROBERTS daughter of Thomas and Elizabeth born 25 December 1751

Anne ROBERTS daughter of Thomas and Elizabeth was born 3 October 1754

William ROBERTS son of Thomas and Elizabeth was born 3 October 1757

Elizabeth ROBERTS daughter of Thomas and ELiz. was born 10 August 1760

Levin HUFFINGTON married Mattilda ACKWORTH 12 November 1753

Angelo HUFFINGTON son of Levin and Mattilda was born 3 January 1757

Charles HUFFINGTON son of Levin and Mattilda was born 10 May 1759

Obediah HUFFINGTON son of Levin and Mattilda was born 11 June 1762

William ANDERSON married Margaret Surman 7 July 1748

William ANDERSON son of William and Margaret was born 9 July 1749

James ANDERSON son of William and Margaret was born 15 April 1751

Isaac ANDERSON son of William and Margaret was born 2 April 1756

Joseph ANDERSON son of William and Margaret was born 15 October 1758

David PRICHARD married Mary HENINGMAN 14 February 1750

John PRICHARD son of David and Mary was born 2 June 1754

David PRICHARD son of David and Mary was born 11 May 1757

James PRICHARD son of David and Mary was born 15 September 1760

William DOUGLAS married Mary ANDERSON 27 September 1758

Samuel DOUGLAS son of William and Mary was born 22 September 1759

Joshua HUMPHRISS married Esther NEAL 28 August 1755

Leah HUMPHRISS daughter of Joshua and Esther was born 14 June 1756

Elijah HUMPHRISS son of Joshua and Esther was born 18 October 1760

Betty DEAN daughter of Charles and Sarah was born 12 April 1748

Levi DEAN son of Charles and Sarah was born 6 November 1753

Noble DEAN son of Charles and Sarah was born 14 February 1755

Abraham DEAN son of Charles and Sarah was born 22 April 1759

Mary DEAN daughter of Charles and Sarah was born 19 February 1752

Peter MALLONE son of Robert and Mary was born 21 January 1738/9

William MALLONE son of Robert and Mary was born 13 July 1741

Thomas MALLONE son of Robert and Mary was born 21 December 1747

John READ married Sarah MALLONE 10 May 1752

Elizabeth READ daughter of John and Sarah was born 15 February 1754

Henny DASHIELL daughter of Thomas and Ann was born 28 January 1758

George DASHIELL son of Thomas and Ann was born 10 September 1759

Patience DASHIELL daughter of Thomas and Ann was born 12 June 1761

William STANFORD married Mary COOPER of Northampton County Virginia, 1 June 1759

John STANFORD son of William and Mary was born 13 May 1760

Nanny STANFORD daughter of William and Mary was born 2 August 1762

Leah COLLINS daughter of Thomas and Rebecka was born 16 November 1764

William STEWART son of Alexander and Rebecca was born 14 February 1738

Samuel ADAMS married Rebecka WHITTINGHAM 1 May 1756

Samuel ADAMS son of Samuel and Rebecka was born 28 February 1756

Leah ADAMS daughter of Samuel and Rebecka was born 5 January 1757

Christiana ADAMS daughter of Samuel and Rebecka born 5 February 1759

Alexander ADAMS son of Samuel and Rebecka was born 13 November 1761

John Whittingham ADAMS son of Samuel and Rebecka born 5 March 1763

Tubman DASHIELL son of George and Arosy was born 17 August 1763

William KIBBLE maried Elizabeth STEWART 24 July 1763

Jonathan JENKINS married Esther HILLMAN 5 August 1761

Ezekiel JENKINS son of Jonathan and Esther was born 12 May 1762

Rachel JENKINS daughter of Jonathan and Esther was born 28 March 1764

Levin COLLINS son of Elizabeth was born 1 May 1764

Elizabeth STEWART daughter of Isabel was born 6 October 1761

John PIPER son of William married Ann PIPER daughter of Christopher on 18 February 1748

Joseph PIPER son of John and Ann was born 8 February 1756

John PIPER son of William married Agnes FINNEY daughter of William on 5 May 1758

Sarah PIPER daughter of John and Agnes was born 14 February 1762

Mary PIPER daughter of John and Agnes was born 4 october 1763

Benjamin Frederick Augustus Ceasar DASHIELL son of Joseph and Martha was born 22 May 1763

Eleanor BIGLANDS daughter of Richard and Mary was born 14 June 1764

George GOSLEE son of John and Hannah was born 12 June 1763

Emma KIBBLE daughter of William and Elizabeth was born 27 April 1764

Samuel CALLAWAY married Mary PRICE 12 April 1762

Rhoda CALLAWAY daughter of Samuel and Mary was born 14 April 1763

William ADAMS son of Samuel and Rebecka was born 18 September 1764

Francis MADDUX married Elizabeth BIGLANDS 26 August 1757

Lazarus MADDUX son of Francis and Elizabeth was born 6 February 1759

Leah MADDUX daughter of Francis and Elizabeth was born 25 July 1761

George NOBLE son of Mary was born 31 March 1762

Mary BOUNDS daughter of Richard Stevens and Mary born 7 October 1764

Salathiel GRIFFIN married Nancy OWENS 10 March 1760

Sinah GRIFFIN daughter of Salathiel and Nancy born 12 December 1760

Nanny GRIFFIN daughter of Salathiel and Nancy was born 21 May 1764

Anna MORRIS daughter of John and Mary was born 29 July 1759

Isaac MORRIS son of John and Mary was born 18 June 1761

Tempe MORRIS daughter of John and Mary was born 1 April 1764

Margaret DASHIELL daughter of Isaac and Henrietta born 1 April 1764

James BOUNDS son of Jonathan and Frances was born 22 February 1741

Mary Ann MORRIS daughter of Joseph and Elisabeth born 5 April 1764

Esther STANFORD daughter of William and Mary was born 6 June 1764

Peter PARSONS son of Peter and Mary was born 10 January 1681

Peter PARSONS married Ursulla JENKINS 2 May 1703

Peter PARSONS son of Peter and Ursulla was born 10 March 1707

George PARSONS son of Peter and Ursulla was born 5 August 1708

George PARSONS married Hannah STEVENS 1 December 1732

William PARSONS son of George and Hannah was born 1 August 1733

George PARSONS son of George and Hannah was born1 6 December 1737

Jonathan PARSONS son of George and Hannah was born 31 May 1739

Abigail PARSONS daughter of George and Hannah was born 20 August 1741

Sarah PARSONS daughter of George and Hannah was born 8 November 1746

William PARSONS married Hannah HEARN 6 January 1757

Samuel PARSONS son of William and Hannah was born 7 November 1757

Betty PARSONS daughter of William and Hannah was born 13 March 1761

Hannah PARSONS daughter of William and Hannah was born 29 July 1764

George PARSONS married Temperance SHERMAN 29 January 1762

Jordan PARSONS son of George and Temperance was born 9 January 1762

Nelly PARSONS daughter of George and Temperance born 24 January 1764

Jonathan PARSONS married Sarah MILLS 31 January 1759

Levin PARSONS son of Jonathan and Sarah was born 26 June 1759

Nancy PARSONS daughter of Jonathan and Sarah was born 31 December 1763

David MEGEE married Mary MacGLAMERY 31 October 1745

Davis MEGEE son of David and Mary was born 19 November 1746

Moses MEGEE son of David and Mary was born 13 December 1748

Leah MEGEE daughter of David and Mary was born 14 December 1750

Nelly MEGEE daughter of David and Mary was born 13 May 1752

Ruben MEGEE son of David and Mary was born 13 February 1754

Josiah MEGEE son of David and Mary was born 16 November 1757

Ann Mary MEGEE daughter of David and Mary was born 19 January 1761

Betty MEGEE daughter of David and Mary was bon 4 March 1763

David MEGEE son of David and Mary was born 12 March 1765

Henry LOWES Jr. son of Henry and Easther married Easther DASHIELL 31 July 1759

Tubman LOWES son of Henry Jr. and Easther born at Quantico 24 September 1764

Mitchel DASHIELL son of Thomas was married to Marget BOHN 16 October 1743

Jean DASHIELL daughter of Mitchell and Marget born 2 September 1744

Thomas DASHIELL son of Mitchell and Marget was born 10 August 1746

Persilah DASHIELL daughter of Mitchell and Marget born 7 October 1748

Mitchel DASHIELL son of Mitchel and Marget was born 22 November 1750

Betty DASHIELL daughter of Mitchell and Marget born 28 November 1752

Sarah DASHIELL daughter of Mitchel and Marget born 16 February 1755

Robert DASHIELL son of Mitchell and Marget was born 10 February 1757

Nancey DASHIELL daughter of Mitchell and Marget was born 4 May 1759

Ragus DASHIELL daughter of Mitchell and Marget born 18 October 1763

Robert ROBERTSON son of Alexander and Leah was born 1 July 1765/6, and died 27 December 1766.

John DASHIELL son of George and Rosey was born 31 October 1765

Josiah Dashiell son of George and Rosey was born 13 January 1768

Leavin LARAMORE married Mary ONEAL 28 September 1762

John LARAMORE son of Leavin and Mary was born 21 September 1763

Mary HUFFINGTON daughter of Lazarus and Mary was born 8 Nov. 1766

Benjamin GILLIS married Easther BYRD 12 December 1765

Leavin GILLIS son of Benjamin and Easter was born 7 February 1767

Thomas BEARD married Sarah BOARDMAN daughter of Graves on 14 November 1762

Mary BEARD daughter of Thomas and Sarah was born 5 January 1763

Jean DASHIELL daughter of Thomas and Jean was born 13 May 1761

Betty DASHIELL daughter of Thomas and Jean was born 22 July 1763

Thomas DASHIELL son of Thomas and Jean was born 14 April 1765

Levin DASHIELL son of Thomas and Jean was born 8 April 1767

David WILLIAMS married Marthew HOULDBROOK 20 August 1766

Thomas WILLIAMS son of David and Marthew was born 28 August 1768

Robert ROBERTSON son of Alexander and Leah was born 2 March 1768

Marting GRIFFEN son of Salathiel and Nancey was born 6 June 1768

Mary Evans COLLIER daughter of Nicholas Evans and Rebeccah was born 25 December 1761

Rebecca COLLIER daughter of Nicholas Evans and Rebeccah was born 21 February 1765

George BENNET son of William and Dority was born 21 February 1765

Elizabeth BENNETT daughter of Wm. and Dority was born 25 March 1768

Betts COLLIER son of Robert and Bridget was born 23 February 1746/7

Doubty COLLIER son of Robert and Bridget was born 14 May 1750

Leah COLLIER daughter of Robert and Bridget was born 9 December 1748/9

Lervezer COLLIER daughter of Robert and Bridget born 2 February 1752

John Nicholson COLLIER son of Robert and Bridget born 14 March 1764

Nelly COLLIER daughter of Robert and Bridget was born 8 June 1766

Henry DASHIELL son of Thomas and Jean was born 9 February 1744

Mary FOUNTAIN daughter of Marsy and Elizabeth born 26 September 1751

William DASHIELL married Mary FOUNTAIN 25 September 1768

Josiah CROCKETT son of John and Mary was born 11 April 1749

Elihu MEZICK son of Jacob and Elizabeth was born 24 June 1716

Delilah MEZICK daughter of Elihu and Sarah was born 17 March 1740

Cattron MEZICK daughter of Elihu and Sarah was born 5 September 1742

James MEZICK son of Elihu and Sarah was born 11 January 1744

Elizabeth MEZICK daughter of Elihu and Sarah was born 5 June 1747

Fischer MEZICK son of Elihu and Sarah FISHER daughter of Henry FISHER and Mary FISHER was born 13 March 1754

Elihu MEZICK son of Elihu and Margret RICHEY daughter of Archibald Richey and Elizabeth, was born 20 March 1756

Sarah MEZICK daughter of Elihu and Margret was born 1 January 1758

Mary MEZICK daughter of Elihu and Margret was born 21 February 1760

John Richey MEZICK son of Elihu and Margret was born 16 February 1762

Daniel MEZICK son of Elihu and Margret was born 16 June 1764

Amillah MEZICK daughter of Elihu and Margret was born 23 June 1766

Susannah MEZICK daughter of Elihu and Margret was born 8 October 1768

Barbary MacCABE daughter of Jesse and Mary was born 16 September 1749

Daniel RICHIE married Deliah MEZICK 27 June 1762

Elizabeth RICHIE daughter of Daniel and Deliah born 6 November 1764

Sarah RICHIE daughter of Daniel and Deliah was born 16 September 1765

Daniel RICHIE son of Daniel and Deliah was born 17 May 1768

Daniel RICHIE son of Daniel and Deliah died 3 July 1768

Margret RICHIE daughter of Daniel and Deliah was born 28 July 1769

Elijah LARIMORE son of James and Elizabeth was born 15 February 1747

Elijah LARIMORE married Cathrine MEZICK 8 April 1766

James LARIMORE son of Elijah and Cathrine was born 26 April 1769

Elizabeth LARIMORE daughter of Elijah and Catherine born 4 March 1767

Elizabeth RICHEY wife of Archibald died 15 November 1761

James RICHEY son of Archibald and Elizabeth died 17 August 1746

James BEARD son of Lewis and Rachel was born 1 January 1747

William ELINSWORTH married Rachel BEARD 25 March 1750

Elizabeth ELINSWORTH daughter of William and Rachel born 13 Feb. 1751

Israel ELINSWORTH son of William and Rachel was born 27 August 1752

Aaron ELINSWORTH son of William and Rachel was born 5 April 1756

Diana ELINSWORTH daughter of Wm. and Rachel was born 9 March 1758

Covinton ELINSWORTH son of Wm. and Rachel was born 28 December 1762

Dolly ELINSWORTH daughter of Wm. and Rachel was born 17 June 1766

Robert ELINSWORTH son of William and Rachel was born 18 December 1768

Daniel RICHEY son of Archibald and Elizabeth born 18 February 1743/4

David DUTTON married Betheir BIBBONS 17 September 1766

Nancy DUTTON daughter of David and Bethier was born 7 August 1768

Levin FLETCHER married Mary MADDUX 15 December 1764

John FLETCHER son of Levin and Mary was born 12 October 1766

Levin FLETCHER son of Levin and Mary was born 9 August 1768

Mary NICHOLSON daughter of Joseph and Sarah was born 17 March 1759

Peggy NICHOLSON daughter of Joseph and Sarah was born 5 October 1760

Levin WALTER married Sarah NICHOLSON, widow 10 January 1766

George Dashiell WALTER son of Levin and Sarah was born 16 April 1766

Easther WALTER daughter of Levin and Sarah was born 9 February 1768

Prissey WALTER daughter of Levin and Sarah was born 9 April 1770

George DASHIELL Sr. died 5 February 1768

Elisha PHILLIPS son of William and Margaret was born 1 June 1769

John NELMS married Nancy WILLIAMS 29 December 1768

William Roberds NELMS son of John and Nancy was born 17 December 1770

John McINTYRE son of Daniel and Elizabeth was born 15 September 1758

Daniel McINTYRE son of Daniel and Elizabeth was born 26 January 1762

James McINTYRE son of Daniel and Elizabeth was born 6 September 1765

Isaac HOPKINS son of Isaac and Margaret was born 24 February 1763

William DORMAN married Sarah BYRD 15 November 1764

Betty DORMAN daughter of William and Sarah was born 8 September 1765

Hezekiah DORMAN son of William and Sarah was born 7 June 1768

William Byrd DORMAN son of William and Sarah was born 24 April 1771

Nathaniel DIXON married Ann PIPER 31 December 1769

Ambrus Piper DIXON son of Nathaniel and Ann was born 9 February 1771

Chaplin CONWAY son of John Span and Susannah was born 22 April 1766

John CONWAY son of John Span and Susannah was born 4 October 1769

James CONWAY son of John Span and Susannah was born 24 February 1772

James DASHIELL son of William and Mary was born 20 September 1771

Joseph DASHIELL son of William and Mary was born 1 February 1772

George FURBUSH son of Peter and Easther was born 22 March 1749

Ephraim VAUGHAN married Eizabeth COOPER 28 February 1752

William VAUGHAN son of Ephraim and Elizabeth was born 3 December 1752

James VAUGHAN son of Ephriam and Elizabeth was born 17 January 1755

Levin VAUGHAN son of Ephraim and Elizabeth was born 10 December 1757

Sarah VAUGHAN daughter of Ephraim and Eliza. was born 3 February 1759

Ellinor VAUGHAN daughter of Ephraim and Eliza. born 4 December 1760

Ephraim VAUGHAN son of Ephraim and Elizabeth was born 6 December 1763

Jonathan VAUGHAN son of Ephraim and Elizabeth born 17 February 1765

Jane VAUGHAN daughter of Ephraim and Elizabeth was born 14 March 1768

Elizabeth VAUGHAN daughter of Ephraim and Eliza. born 2 November 1770

Isaac VAUGHAN son of Ephraim and Elizabeth was born 14 October 1772

Ephraim VAUGHAN Sr. died 27 March 1773

Martha MEZICK daughter of Elihu and Margret was born 29 March 1773

Littleton ROBERTSON son of Alexander and Leah was born 4 April 1770

Alexander ROBERTSON son of Alexander and Leah born 17 February 1772

Isaac ROBERTSON son of Alexander and Leah was born 29 December 1762
and died 20 January 1763

Jesse ROBERTSON son of Alexander and Leah was born 23 October 1764

Mitchel ROBERTSON son of William and Sarah was born 14 February 1767

Samuel ROBERTSON son of William and Sarah was born 12 February 1770

Edward KILLUM married Priscilla TAYLOR 20 January 1772

Ann KILLUM daughter of Edward and Priscilla was born 3 November 1772

Peter DASHIELL son of Robert and Isabell was born 1 March 1771

Mary ACWORTH daughter of Henry and Mary was born 23 October 1744

James PHILLIPS and Mary ACWORTH married 28 March 1762

Henry PHILLIPS son of James and Mary was born 4 December 1762

Nelly PHILLIPS daughter of James and Mary was born 25 December 1764

Ann PHILLIPS daughter of James and Mary was born 27 October 1769

Robert Givans PHILLIPS son of James and Mary was born 20 December 1772

Charles HARRIS married Mary GREEN 23 January 1772

George HARRIS son of Charles and Mary was born 9 February 1773

Elizabeth STEWART wife of John died 2 February 1774

Benjamin WAILES son of John and Eunice was born 14 February 1756

Ann WAILES daughter of John and Eunice was born 8 September 1758

Charles WAILES son of John and Eunice was born 11 August 1762

Mary Hart WAILES daughter of John and Eunice was born 16 October 1764

Easther WAILES daughter of John and Eunice was born 13 June 1768

Elizabeth WAILES daughter of John and Eunice was born 7 March 1774

Suckey DUTTON daughter of David and Bethier was born 14 March 1771

Bethyer DUTTON daughter of David and Bethyer was born 20 January 1774

Capt. George McCLESTER married Mary TOWNSEND 28 February 1753

Sarah McCLESTER daughter of George and Mary was born 14 April 1755

Rachel McCLESTER daughter of George and Mary was born 17 October 1757

Charles SMITH married Mary MCCLESTER, widow of Capt. George on 2 October 1760

Thomas SMITH son of Charles and Mary was born 28 January 1761

James SMITH son of Charles and Mary was born 22 November 1763

Benjamin SMITH son of Charles and Mary was born 2 January 1768

Nelley SMITH daughter of Charles and Mary was born 26 May 1771

Michael THARP married Eunice COOPER 1 January 1772

William THARP son of Michael and Eunice was born 28 October 1772

James McMurray JONES married Prissey DORMAN 21 December 1759

Mary JONES daughter of James and Prissey was born 13 January 1760

Robert JONES son of James and Prissey was born 26 February 1770

Sarah JONES daughter of James and Prissey was born 26 September 1772

Jonathan STANFORD married Grace PHILLIPS 28 June 1767

Josiah STANFORD son of Jonathan and Grace was born 10 August 1771

George JONES son of William, ship carpenter and Sarah was born 8 November 1753.

John KITTNAM son of Edward and Priscilla was born 13 December 1774

Anne ROBERTSON daughter of William and Sarah was born 5 June 1774

John EVANS Jr. married Sarah DASHIELL 26 May 1773

Ann Dashiell EVANS daughter of John Jr. and Sarah born 13 March 1774

Levy HOPKINS married Betty NICHOLSON 8 November 1772

Linny HOPKINS daughter of Levy and Betty was born 6 February 1774

George HOPKINS son of Levy and Betty 31 October 1775

Robert Hunter MORRIS son of Joseph and Elizabeth 25 March 1769

Elizabeth MORRIS daughter of Joseph and Elizabeth was born 2 May 1772

Archabld DASHIELL son of Robert and Isabelle was born 3 March 1773

Sarah DASHIELL son of Robert and Isabelle was born 3 December 1775

George HANDY the eldest son of Isaac and Ann married Nelly GILLIS 9 February 1755

Leah HANDY daughter of George and Nelly was born 2 October 1757

Isaac HANDY son of George and Nelly was born 9 March 1762

William HANDY son of George and Nelly was born 6 January 1765

Ann HANDY son of George and Nelly was born 5 September 1767

Nelly HANDY daughter of George and Nelly was born 7 March 1770

Elizabeth HANDY daughter of George and Nelly was born 8 June 1775

Outerbridge HORSEY son of William and Elinor was born 5 March 1775

Benjamin HERON son of William and Elizabeth was born 27 May 1727

Elijah HERON son of William and Elizabeth was born 13 Mach 1729

Elijah HERON married Sarah JOHNSON 14 November 1754

William HERON son of Elijah and Sarah was born 28 October 1755

Joanna HERON daughter of Elijah and Sarah was born 4 December 1757

Matty DASHIELL daughter of Matthias and Mary was born 18 May 1777

Stephen BENNETT son of William and Dorithy was born 1 August 1771

Joseph WRIGHT son of Jacob and Betty was born 2 February 1771

Benjamin WRIGHT son of Jacob and Betty was born 21 July 1773

James DASHIELL married Sarah EVANS 14 September 1763

Mary DASHIELL daughter of James and Sarah was born 5 July 1764

Jane DASHIELL daughter of James and Sarah was born 27 August 1766

Sarah DASHIELL daughter of James and Sarah was born 5 February 1770

Jesse DASHIELL son of James and Sarah was born 16 February 1772

Susanna DASHIELL daughter of James and Sarah was born 7 March 1774

Betty DASHIELL daughter of James and Sarah was born 1 June 1776

Stephen MALLONE son Robert was born 8 June 1770

Mary MALLONE daughter of Robert was born 13 March 1775

William MALLONE son of Robert was born 9 June 1777

Samuel JACKSON married Alice CROCKETT 24 April 1754

Amelia JACKSON daughter of Samuel and Alice was born 20 December 1756

Mary JACKSON daughter of Samuel and Alice was born 21 April 1760

Alice JACKSON wife of Samuel died 8 December 1760

Samuel JACKSON married Patience WRIGHT 27 May 1762

Rachel JACKSON daughter of Samuel and Patience was born 13 Feb. 1763

Jonathan JACKSON son of Samuel and Patience was born 7 May 1765

Easther JACKSON daughter of Samuel and Patience was born 13 July 1769

Ellinor JACKSON daughter of Samuel and Patience was born 5 Feb. 1772

Priscilla JACKSON daughter of Samuel and Patience born 1 December 1777

Nancy JACKSON daughter of Samuel and Patience was born 26 March 1779

Prissey JONES daughter of James McMurray and Prissey was born 14 February 1777.

James WALTER son of Levin and Sarah was born 28 November 1771

Sarah WALTER daughter of Levin and Sarah was born 21 April 1774

William CONNERLY son of Thomas and Margret was born 18 October 1764

Bridget CONNERLY daughter of Thomas and Margret born 29 October 1767

John CONNERLY son of Thomas and Margret was born 4 July 1770

Elijah CONNERLY son of Thomas and Margret was born 29 August 1772

William BEDSWOTTH son of Thomas and Susanna was born 15 August 1764

John RENCHER son of William and Martha was born 7 January 1754

Margaret RENCHER daughter of Wm. and Martha was born 4 November 1759

Sarah RENCHER daughter of William and Martha was born 15 March 1763

Isaac GILES son of Jacob and Eunice was born 13 July 1762

William GILES son of Jacob and Eunice was born 16 September 1768

William DASHIELL son of W. and Mary was born 3 February 1779

Daniel PHILLIPS married to Ann (no name) 2 November 1756

Amelia PHILLIPS daughter of Daniel and Ann was born 22 May 1758

Mary PHILLIPS daughter of Daniel and Ann was born 20 April 1760

Richard PHILLIPS son of Daniel and Ann was born 3 June 1762

Daniel PHILLIPS son of Daniel and Ann was born 24 July 1764

John PHILLIPS son of Daniel and Ann was born 7 April 1767

Nancy PHILLIPS daughter of Daniel and Ann was born 3 May 1769

James PHILLIPS son of Daniel and Ann was born 22 January 1774

Joshua PHILLIPS son of Daniel and Ann was born 16 November 1775

Thomas PHILLIPS son of Daniel and Ann was born 29 November 1777

Robert Handy DASHIELL son of George and Priscilla born 11 July 1766

Priscilla DASHIELL daughter of George and Priscilla born 26 April 1768

George DASHIELL son of George and Priscilla was born 26 May 1770

Daniel Jones DASHIELL son of George and Prisc. born 4 January 1773

John DASHIELL son of George and Priscilla was born 17 April 1775

Richard STEPHENS son of Stephen was born 25 February 1762

Tempy STEPHENS daughter of Stephen was born 19 November 1769

John STEPHENS son of Stephen was born 7 October 1771

Samuel STEPHENS son of Stephen was born 28 April 1774

Ephraim ACWORTH son of Samuel was born 17 October 1759

Clement FLOYD son of Hugh and Leah was born 14 October 1771

Elizabeth FLOYD daughter of Hugh and Leah was born 9 November 1774

Leah FLOYD daughter of Hugh and Leah was born 11 December 1777

William STEWART married Sarah DASHIELL daughter of Charles and
Elizabeth on 11 December 1760

Betty STEWART daughter of William and Sarah was born 15 May 1762

Rebecca STEWART daughter of William and Sarah born 24 February 1764

John STEWART son of William and Sarah was born 2 December 1766

Sarah King STEWART daughter of Wm. and Sarah was born 22 March 1769

Nelley STEWART daughter of William and Sarah was born 2 August 1771

William STEWART son of William and Sarah was born 14 February 1774

Ephraim King STEWART son of Wm. and Sarah was born 21 January 1779

Cabel JONES son of James Mackmorie and Priscilla born 26 December 1779

Jane STEWART daughter of John and Elizabeth was born 4 September 1771

Alexander STEWART son of John and Elizabeth was born 13 September 1773

William F. DASHIELL son of William and Sarah was born 26 January 1750

Priscilla EVANS daughter of Nicholas and Priscilla born 4 August 1757

William F. DASHIELL and Prise EVANS married 24 August 1775

Ichabod DASHIELL son of William F. and Prise was born 27 February 1777

Francis DASHIELL son of William F. and Prise was born 1 July 1779

Rebecca DASHIELL died 3 May 1769

Capt. CHARLES Dashiell died 11 March 1761

Ephraim KING died 12 July 1777

Elizabeth DASHIELL wife of Charles died 19 July 1770

Samuel KING married Elizabeth WAGGAMAN 2 September 1779

Richard KENNETT son of John and Margret was born 26 June 1773

Matthias DASHIELL married Mary HOPKINS 25 January 1775

Ephraim King STEWART died 27 June 1780, age 17 months, 5 days.

Ann STEWART daughter of William and Sarah was born 6 June 1781

Elizabeth VENABLES daughter of Benjamin and Betty born 22 Feb. 1765

Charles VENABLES son of Benjamin and Betty was born 19 December 1767

Robert VENABLES son of Benjamin and Betty was born 7 April 1769

Ann VENABLES daughter of Benjamin and Betty was born 14 June 1771

Sarah Dashiell VENABLES daughter of Benj. & Betty born 20 July 1773

Leah VENABLES daughter of Benjamin and Betty was born 24 March 1776

Peggy Washington VENABLES daughter of Benj. & Betty born 17 July 1778

Abraham TAYLOR son of William and Sarah was born 5 March 1726/7

Abraham TAYLOR married Mary _____ 17 May 1751

Bartholomew TAYLOR son of Abraham and Mary was born 27 February 1756

Abraham TAYLOR son of Abraham and Mary was born 7January 1772

William TAYLOR son of Abraham and Mary was born 4 April 1775

Lowder TAYLOR son of Abraham and Mary was born 19 October 1776

Priscilla EVANS daughter of John of Neh.and Sarah born 7 November 1778

William HORSEY son of William and Eliner was born 16 May 1780

Thomas LEATHERBURY son of John and Elinor was born 19 March 1742

Thomas LEATHERBURY and Ann TAYLOR were married 5 January 1771

John LEATHERBURY son of Thomas and Ann was born 4 February 1772

Perry LEATHERBURY son of Thomas and Ann was born 18 January 1776

Catherine RICHIE daughter of Daniel and Delie born 10 February 1772

Archable RICHIE, a cochman died 11 November 1778

Hugh FLOYD son of Hugh and Leah was born 16 March 1780

Peggy GILES daughter of Isaac and Elizabeth was born 6 October 1764

Anney GILES daughter of Isaac and Elizabeth was born 28 July 1771

Thomas GILES son of Isaac and Elizabeth was born 14 January 1776

Sarah GILES daughter of Isaac and ELizabeth was born 19 July 1778

Jesse BYRD married Mary RECORDS 3 October 1771

Nancy BYRD daughter of Jesse and Mary was born 25 February 1774

Thomas BYRD son of Jesse and Mary was born 22 September 1777

James BYRD son of Jesse and Mary was born 24 January 1780

Lemee RECORDS married Sophia BYRD 9 April 1762

Lemee RECORDS son of Lemee and Sophia was born 27 January 1763

Amelia RECORDS daughter of Lemee and Sophia was born 3 November 1766

Sophrah RECORDS daughter of Lemee and Sophia was born 21 December 1769

Thomas RECORDS son of Lemee and Sophia was born 10 December 1772

Polly RECORDS daughter of Lemee and Sophia was born 16 October 1775

Sarah RECORDS daughter of Lemee and Sophrah was born 20 September 1779

William HORSEY son of William and Elender was born 16 May 1780

Alexander PORTER son of William and Ann was born 29 March 1771

George JONES son of James McMorey and Prissey was born 23 Feb. 1782

Joseph DASHIELL son of George and Elizabeth was born 17 November 1755

Joseph DASHIELL Jr. married Jeane EVANS 25 August 1779

Nancy DASHIELL daughter of Joseph and Jeane was born 1 October 1780

Charles WEATHERLY son of James and Major was born 5 March 1749

Charles WEATHERLY married Marget KILBORN 24 February 1774

Sarah WEATHERLY daughter of Charles and Marget born 19 October 1776

James WEATHERLY son of Charles and Marget was born 4 January 1779

William HOPKINS son of Levi and Elizabeth was born 17 September 1780

Isaac HOPKINS son of Levi and Elizabeth was born 10 April 1785

Andrew MURFFEY married Anne RIGHT, widow 26 November 1768

Andrew MURFFEY was born at the Casle of Cortbrow Illand eldest son of John O. MURFEY, Inda 1717

Bette MURFFEY daughter of Andrew and Anne was born 23 December 1773

George AIRS son of Jacob and Sarah was born 17 September 1746

Amelia JONES daughter of William and Prisila was born 8 December 1755

Jacob AIRS father of George, died 31 March 1767

George AIRS married Amelia JONES 23 March 1774

Priscilla AIRS daughter of George and Amelia was born 12 January 1775

Littleton AIRS son of George and Amelia was born 16 August 1776

Matley STEWART daughter of William and Sarah was born 14 October 1783

Sarah AIRS daughter of George and Amelia was born 16 December 1777

George AIRS son of George and Amelia was born 5 July 1779

Martha AIRS daughter of George and Amelia was born 22 September 1780

53

Joshua E. MOOR married Isabella HICKMAN 22 September 1768

Betty E. MOOR daughter of Joshua and Isabella born 12 February 1769

Nicholas E. MOOR son of Joshua E. and Isabella born 28 August 1771

Joshua E. MOOR son of Joshua and Isabella was born 27 August 1773

Jonathan E. MOOR son of Joshua and Isabella was born 27 September 1775

Samuel E. MOOR son of Joshua and Isabella was born 12 July 1777

Thomas E. MOOR son of Joshua and Isabella was born 6 November 1778

Isabella E. MOOR daughter of Joshua and Isabella born 20 Nov. 1780

Ann VENABLES wife of Benjamin died 2 January 1782

Benjamin VENABLES husband of Ann died on the last day of the same
month 1782, and had been married 52 years.

Joseph VENABLES son of Benjamin and Betty was born 5 June 1782

Israel ELINSWORTH married Priscilla ELIOTT 5 April 1777

Rachel ELINSWORTH daughter of Israel and Priscilla born 19 July 1777

Rodey Eliott ELINSWORTH daughter of Israel & Prisc. born 29 Nov.1779

Priscilla ELINSWORTH wife of Israel died 8 March 1780

Israel ELINSWORTH married Barbara McCABE 1 February 1782

Jesse ELINSWORTH son of Israel and Barbary was born 13 March 1782

William BALLARD son of Charles and Mathew was born 3 November 1773

Matthew MEZICK daughter of Elihu and Margret was born 29 March 1773

Ritchie KINNE son of Solomon and Sarah was born 4 April 1782

Mitchell DASHIELL son of Mitch married Mary HURT 29 February 1779

Robert DASHIELL son of Mitchell and Mary was born 28 July 1779

James DISHAROON married Sarah DORITY 9 November 1775

Prissa DISHAROON daughter of James and Sarah was born 24 June 1776

John DISHAROON son of James and Sarah was born 27 October 1777

James DISHAROON son of James and Sarah was born 22 January 1779

William DISHAROON son of James and Sarah was born 1 May 1781

Nancey DISHAROON daughter of James and Sarah was born 13 April 1783

Samuel King JONES son of James and Priscilla was born 11 January 1784

James Ma. JONES married Sarah ROE daughter of Nicholas 8 August 1785

Mary Day JONES daughter of Matthias and Nancy born 19 November 1774

Nancy JONES wife of Mathias died 19 January 1777

Samuel DASHIELL son of Joseph and Jeane was born 20 December 1782

Lorry DASHIELL son of William F. and Priscilla born 15 November 1781

Jones BOUNDS married Elizabeth RICHARDSON 16 May 1778

James BOUNDS son of Jones and Elizabeth was born 28 March 1779

Mary BOUNDS daughter of Jones and ELizabeth was born 21 October 1782

John JONES son of Benjamin and ELizabeth was born 11 February 1757

Betsey JONES wife of John was born 27 June 1762

John JONES and Betsey DASHIELL married 20 September 1780

Nelly JONES daughter of John and Betsey was born 17 October 1781

Benjamin JONES son of John and Betsey was born 17 May 1783

Levin WALTER son of Levin and Sarah was born 8 July 1779

Solomon KENNEY married Sarah MEZICK 1 June 1780

Richey KENNEY son of Solomon and Sarah was born 4 April 1783

Elizabeth Turpon KINNEY daughter of Solomon & Sarah born 14 Jan. 1784

Daniel WAILES son of Joseph and Marget was born 18 September 1780

John WAILES son of Joseph and Marget was born 22 September 1782

William COLLINS son of Thomas and Rebecca married Emme KIBBLE 10 October 1782

Nancy Steward COLLINS son of Wm. and Emme was born 15 August 1783

William COLLINS son of William and Emme was born 12 January 1785

Thomas SMITH married Mary DASHIELL 5 September 1785

George Collier HOPKINS married Betty LEATHERBURY 27 August 1761

Prisse HOPKINS daughter of George C. and Betty was born 8 Jan. 1762

John HOPKINS son of George C. and Betty was born 25 December 1765

Jeans HOPKINS daughter of George C. and Betty was born 7 December 1767

Liexzan HOPKINS daughter of George C. and Betty was born 6 March 1770

Matha HOPKINS daughter of George C. and Betty was born 27 January 1772

Roger HOPKINS son of George C. and Betty was born 9 January 1774

Mitchel HOPKINS son of George C. and Betty was born 18 January 1776

Zacheus HOPKINS son of George C. and Betty was born 10 November 1778

George HOPKINS son of George C. and Betty was born 9 December 1780

Elizabeth HOPKINS daughter of George C.& Betty was born 7 January 1783

Elinor HOPKINS daughter of George C. & Betty was born 6 February 1786

Betty HOPKINS wife of George Collier died 6 February 1786

Jesse DASHIELL died 7 June 1778

Jane ROBERTSON daughter of James and Jane was born 5 May 1770

John STEWART Jr. married Jane ROBERTSON 27 July 1786

Elihu LARRAMORE married Mary DUGLAS 4 March 1782

Nelly Duglas LARRAMORE daughter of Elihu and Mary born 21 October 1784

Reuben LARRAMORE son of Elihu and Mary was born 31 April 1787

Peggy Nicholson HOPKINS daughter of Levi and Betty born 11 Nov. 1786

Robert STEWART son of William and Sarah was born 27 January 1788

Elizabeth NELSON daughter of William and Ann born 26 September 1735

Elizabeth NELSON married Isaac ATKINSON 7 Mary 1757

William ATKINSON son of Isaac and Elizabeth was born 23 February 1758

Joshua ATKINSON son of Isaac and Elizabeth was born 6 June 1759

Nanney ATKINSON daughter of Isaac and Elizab. born 28 September 1760

Betty ATKINSON daughter of Isaac and Elizabeth was born 2 July 1763

Leah JONES daughter of James McMurray and Sarah born 2 June 1785

Nicholson JONES son of James Mc. and Sarah was born 9 December 1788

Mary Dashiell HOPKINS daughter of Levi and Betty was born 16 June 1791

William DASHIELL of Tipqueen died 7 January 1792

Phillip COVINGTON married Prissey NICHOLSON 26 February 1778

John COVINGTON son of Phillip and Prissey was born 13 March 1779

Polly COVINGTON daughter of Phillip and Prissey born 22 January 1781

Phillip COVINGTON son of Phillip and Prissey was born 12 March 1783

Nelly COVINGTON daughter of Phillip and Prissey born 5 February 1785

Abel COVINGTON son of Phillip and Prissey was born 25 February 1788

Hurimer COVINGTON son of Phillip and Prissey was born 12 March 1790

Ephraim WILSON married Easther DASHIELL daughter of Mitchel and Peggy, 1 January 1786

George D. WILSON son of Ephraim and Easther was born 4 November 1786

Jacob MESSICK married Sarah PORTER 25 May 1772

Baptis MESSICK son of Jacob and Sarah was born 13 April 1773

Ketchuel MESSICK daughter of Jacob and Sarah was born 21 Feb. 1775

Joshua Cornwallis MESSICK son of Jacob and Sarah born 9 December 1778

Hart PORTER married Ketchuel MESSICK 17 January 1793

Jacob MESSICK father, died 5 December 1782

Harriot Elizabeth FARRINGTON daughter of Levin and Sarah was born 19 March 1792

Clarerase LANKFORD daughter of Tubman and Betsey born 2 June 1792

Isaac Killem ADAMS son of Angelo and Polly was born 4 June 1792

Samuel PERDUE son of James and Sarah was born 7 June 1792

Elihu LARMORE son of ELihu and Molley was born 8 June 1791

William ANDERSON son of James and Mary was born 8 July 1792

William HEARN son of Benjamin and Matty was born 1 August 1792

Isaac TOADVINE son of Henry and Rhoday was born 4 August 1792

William HUMPHRIS son of Ezekiel and Peggy was born 10 August 1792

Sarah RECORDS daughter of Archelaus and Zepporah born 12 August 1792

Francis MOOR son of Thomas and Elisabeth was born 19 August 1792

James BOUNDS son of William and Bridget was born 5 September 1792

Peggy BENNET daughter of George and Betty was born 12 September 1792

Matty LARMORE daughter of Samuel and Betsy was born 17 September 1792

Winder BAILEY son of Boardwine and Matty was born 19 September 1792

James KENNEDY son of Bartholomew and Nancy was born 21 September 1792

Sarah Lamee WINSOR daughter of William and Euphronia born 28 Sep.1791

Samuel GRAY son of John and Mary was born 6 October 1792

Ebenezer Cotman WALLER son of James Weatherly Waller and Ann was born 6 October 1792

William KIBBLE son of John and Elizabeth was born 10 October 1792

Polley WRIGHT daughter of Handy and Acworth was born 14 October 1792

Mary HUGHS daughter of Jesse and Sarah was born 15 October 1792

Esther GREEN daughter of Ezekiel and Leah was born 5 September 1789

Rachel GREEN daughter of Ezekiel and Leah was born 21 October 1792

Harryett DASHIELL daughter of Arthur Jr. and Esther born 24 Oct. 1792

Peggy Hardy DASHIELL daughter of James and Alleyfair born 25 Oct.1792

Nelly PARKER daughter of John and Scarborough born 28 October 1792

Patty CULVER daughter of Aron and Zillah was born 29 October 1792

Noah SMITH son of Archable and Esther was born 29 October 1792

Thomas HAYMAN son of John and Edee was born 2 November 1792

Peggy BROWN daughter of David and Nancy was born 5 November 1792

Elizabeth Ware CHENEY daughter of Ware and Esther born 11 Nov.1792

Mary COVINGTON daughter of Phillip and Priscilla born 14 November 1792

George PARSONS son of Samuel and Betty was born 26 November 1792

John Jarett DAVIS son of Reuben and Sarah was born 29 November 1792

William WILLIAMS son of William and Salley was born 4 Debember 1791

William BRATTEN son of John and Priscilla was born 4 December 1792

John SUTTON son of William and Rachel was born 7 December 1792

George MOOR son of John and Sarah was born 31 August 1792

Robert CHRISTOPHER and Samuel CHRISTOPHER, twin sons of George and Nancy were born 20 December 1792

Kittura VINSON daughter of Eli and Ann was born 23 March 1792

Patta PHILLIPS daughter of Elijah and Alla was born 25 December 1792

Samuel MITCHEL son of Stephen and Nancy was born 1 January 1793

Sarah HITCH daughter of Elias and Easter was born 2 January 1793

James POLLITT son of James and Esther was born 6 January 1793

Henry Tubman DUGLAS son of William and Jean was born 6 January 1793

ELizabeth SHOCKLEY daughter of John and Cattran was born 19 Jan.1793

Eli PARSONS son of Jordan and Leah was born 21 January 1793

Matty HAYMAN daughter of Nehemiah and Tabby was born 24 January 1793

Benson Bond LOW son of Tubman and Elizabeth BOND was born 2 Feb.1793

Absalom TULLEY son of Benjamin and Ann was born 29 August 1792

Thomas WALLER son of George and Elender was born 29 December 1793

William FOOKES son of Thomas and Lettishea was born 29 January 1793

Thomas TULL son of Jacob and Sarah was born 6 January 1793

Ann INGERSOL daughter of Richard and Elizabeth was born 13 Nov.1792

Leah OWINGS daughter of Samuel and Katty was born 14 January 1793

Sally JONES daughter of George and Sarah was born 27 December 1792

Eleanor Whinright WALLER daughter of Wm. & Rebecca born 11 Jan. 1793

William GOSLING son of William and Charity was born 12 February 1793

Prissey Evans DASHIELL daughter of Joseph and Jane born 15 March 1785

Charles DASHIELL son of Joseph and Jane was born 12 May 1788

Jane DASHIELL wife of Joseph died 17 September 1790

Margaret Jacobs MEZICK daughter of John R. & Nancy born 27 April 1792

Daniel MEZICK son of John R. and Nancy was born 12 May 1794

Mary Jacobs MEZICK daughter of John R. & Nancy was born 12 May 1794

James MILLER son of Isaac and Eunice was born 3 August 1779

George BENNIT married Betty BIRD 21 March 1784

Nancy BENNIT daughter of George and Betty was born 15 January 1785

Henry BENNIT son of George and Betty was born 15 October 1787

Esther BENNIT daughter of George and Betty was born 23 May 1790

Peggy BENNIT daughter of George and Betty was born 12 September 1792

Matthew PORTER son of Joshua and Elizabeth was born 5 August 1795 and baptized 28 January 1796

Nelly HUGHES daughter of Arthur and Elizabeth was born 27 November 1795 and baptized 28 January 1796

Jenny TRAVIS daughter of Meshek and Ann was born 9 December 1795 and baptized 28 January 1796

Sally Jones WATER daughter of John and Betsey was born 18 October 1795 and baptized 28 January 1796

William DASHIELL married Jenney HOPKINS 9 October 1793

George DASHIELL son of William and Jenney was born 18 October 1794

Keturah DASHIELL daughter of William was born 21 October 1786

Leah DASHIELL daughter of William was born 15 December 1788

William DASHIELL son of George and Betty was born 2 February 1760

Nelly DASHIELL daughter of George and Betty was born 6 June 1772

Robert DASHIELL son of George and Betty was born 31 December 1762

Sarah LARMORE daughter of Samuel and Betty was born 8 May 1796

George Washington COLLIER son of George and Martha born 27 Jan. 1796

Molley ENSELY daughter of Denward and Betsey was born 3 September 1797

Jesse WEATHERLY son of James and Polley was born 20 September 1795 and baptized 28 January 1796

Mathew TRAVIS married Priscilla HARRIS 28 January 1796

Priscilla HANDY daughter of Isaac and Priscilla was born 5 April 1795 and baptized 6 March 1796

Nancy CROCKET daughter of Shiles and Martha was born 19 April 1795

Betty DASHIELL daughter of Robert and Rebecca was born 13 November

1796 and baptized 6 March 1797

Elizabeth Sarah Ann DASHIELL daughter of Levin and Priscilla was born 8 September 1796 and baptized 27 October 1796

James EVANS son of James and Betsey was born 9 May 1796 and baptized 2 October 1796

Isaac AIRES son of George and Nancy was born 31 May 1796 and baptized 22 October 1796

James ENSLEY son of William and Delila was born 14 July 1796 and baptized 22 October 1796

Jane NICHOLSON daughter of Thomas and Rebecca was born 7 June 1792

Robert DASHIELL son of George and Betty JONES born 31 December 1762

Robert DASHIELL married Rebeah STEWART daughter of Wm. 14 June 1789

Tubman DASHIELL son of Robert and Rebeah was born 7 August 1791

Sandy DASHIELL son of Robert D. and Rebecca was born 14 August 1793

Betty DASHIELL daughter of Robert and Rebecca born 13 November 1795

Peggy SMITH daughter of Thomas and Mary was born 7 July 1786

Isaac SMITH son of Thomas and Mary was born 28 December 1788

Mary SMITH daughter of Thomas and Mary was born 28 February 1791

Matty COVINGTON daughter of Phillip and Priscilla was born 28 February 1797 and baptized 8 May 1797

Elizabeth Elinor DASHIELL daughter of William and Jenney was born 17 February 1797 and baptized 8 May 1797

Ebenezer COLLIER son of George and Lueazer was born 27 February 1772

Elizabeth WALTER daughter of Benjamin and Jane was born 3 December 1796 and baptized 15 June 1797

Levin RITCHIE son of James and Easther was born 4 July 1794

James RITCHIE son of James and Easther was born 28 February 1797 and baptized 18 June 1797

Nancy CARDIF daughter of Nicholas and Nelly was born 27 June 1797 and baptized 25 August 1797

Zadock MEZICK son of Daniel and Priscilla was born 26 December 1798 and baptized 19 March 1799

William DASHIELL son of Robert and Rebecca was born 3 September 1798 and baptized 19 March 1799

Levin COLLIER son of George and Patty was born 22 August 1798 and baptized 31 March 1799

Nancy Wallace WALTER daughte of William and Priscilla was born 22 August 1798 and baptized 31 March 1799 by Rev. Reece

Sarah Eliza Ann HOPKINS daughter of Isaac and Martha was born 4 January 1799 and baptized 31 March 1799

Benjamin Jones DASHIELL son of Henry and Elizabeth born 22 Nov.1798

Hariet MEZICK daughter of Elihu and Leah was born 27 August 1798

William Luckill GRUMBLE son of George and Ann was born 14 April 1798

Sarah WILSON daughter of Henry and Sarah was born in 1798 and baptized 18 March 1799

Thomas Reddish KNIGHT son of James and Elizabeth was born(no date)

Martha CROCKET daughter of Shiles and Elizabeth was born 25 Sep. 1798

William Acworth TAYLOR son of John and Tempey was born 13 Sep. 1798

John HUGHS son of Arthur and Elizabeth was born 8 March 1798 and baptized 17 June 1798

William PORTER son of Hugh and Peggy was born 3 March 1798 and baptized 18 June 1798

James WINDSOR son of James and Rebecca was born 7 April 1799

Nancy Ann WALTER daughter of John and ELizabeth was born 8 May 1798 and baptized 18 June 1798

Nelly LONG daughter of John LONG and Nelley Weatherly HOPKINS his wife was born 9 April 1798 and baptized 18 June 1798

Jane DICKERSON daughter of Samuel and Jane was born 11 May 1798

Reverend Joshua REECE was born 28 March 1774

Thomas JONES son of Thomas was born 1 January 1772

George AIRES son of George and Amelia was born 3 July 1779

Richard GREEN son of Samuel was born 9 November 1798

Ebenezer ANDERSON son of Joshua and Sarah was born 19 March 1799

James Knight BADLEY son of Richard and Rachel was born 15 Jan. 1799

Nancy CASTON was born 5 September 1798

Levin GRAY son of John and Mary was born 18 January 1799

Peggy RUSSUM daughter of William and Nelly V. K. was born 6 May 1798

George WHITHEAR was born 13 November 1798

Peggy Jones DASHIELL daughter of George and Mary was born 30 Nov. 1798

Leah RELPH daughter of James and Mary was born 13 January 1799

Betty PHILLIPS daughter of Joshua and Mary was born 21 March 1799

Ann MEZICK daughter of James and Bridget was born 18 December 1798 and baptized 31 March 1799

Hyram PORTER was born 1 January 1799

John BARKLEY was born 3 January 1799

Benjamin WALTER son of Benjamin and Jane was born 21 February 1799

James DUNN son of Moses and Susanna was born 10 March 1799

Peter DASHIELL son of Robert and Mary was born 12 January 1799

Leah DUNN daughter of Richard and Mary was born 17 February 1799

Sarah HOPKINS daughter of James and Mary was born 27 December 1799

David HOPKINS son of Susan was born 3 March 1799

Clement STANFORD son of Richard and Esther was born 31 January 1799

William H. WINDER married Gertrude POLK 9 May 1799 by Rev.Thos.Scott

Levin PARSONS son of Samuel and Betty was born 18 April 1799

James ACWORTH son of Richard and Elizabeth was born 6 September 1798

William Patrick CULVER son of Jesse and Margaret born in Jan. 1798

William HITCH son of William E. and Polly was born 14 March 1799

Clement HULL son of Edward and Sinea was born 29 December 1798

Nancy Lassett STERLING daughter of John and Rachel born 14 April 1799

Eleanor TULLEY daughter of John and Ann was born 6 January 1799

Henrietta BIRCKHEAD daughter of William and Sarah born 28 July 1799

William Hamilton CHAILLE son of Wm. and Ann was born 1 March 1799

John Phillips GILES son of Isaac and Nelley was born 6 May 1799

James Russel GREEN son of Samuel and Rachel was born 24 April 1799

Levin BENNETT son of Levin and Elizabeth was born 18 January 1799

Mathias BENNETT was born 27 June 1799

Percy WALTER son of Robert and Priscilla was born 21 March 1799

Henry WILSON son of William and Nancy was born 3 September 1799

William TURPIN son of Denwood and Mary was born 7 December 1799

Relph CARTER son of Robert and Ann was born 11 March 1799

Elizabeth THOMASON daughter of Ezekiel and Rachel born 26 October 1796

Pitt DASHIELL son of Arthur and Esther was born 24 March 1799

Polly INGRAM daughter of Samuel and Priscilla was born 16 Feb. 1799

John Henry CULVER son of John was born 14 April 1799

Mary SHOCKLEY daughter of John was born 7 January 1799

Obed BAYLY son of Obed and Leah was born 20 March 1799

Newton BAYLY son of Boardwine and Matty was born 31 March 1798

William SHOCKLEY son of John was born 9 October 1797

James BOTHAM son of John and Polly was born 27 October 1798

Eli BENNETT son of Joshua was born 7 April 1799

Samuel Hudson REVELL son of George and Jane was born 18 January 1799

Robert MALLONE son of Stephen and Elizabeth was born 17 September 1799

Hannah Watson RUKE daughter of Joseph and Mary was born 10 March 1799

Perry OLEPHINT son of William and Lidy was born 23 September 1798

Elinor COX daughter of John and Elinor was born 30 March 1799

George D. ATKINSON son of Isaac and Elizabeth was born 2 October 1776

William Smallwood RICHARDSON son of Wm. and Mary was born 17 Aug. 1799

Mitchel DORMAN son of Jesse and Peggy was born 3 November 1799

Charlotte FAREINGTON daughter of Levin and Sarah was born 19 Sep. 1797

Nelley DORMAN daughter of Mathias and Sarah was born 20 April 1799

Jesse PARMORE son of James and Polley was born 21 June 1799

Isaac ENNIS son of Outen and Polley was born 26 March 1799

William Adams McGRATH son of John and Nancy was born 10 May 1799

Elizabeth Martain BAKER daughter of John and Sarah born 9 June 1799

William CURRY was born 28 March 1799

Betsey LARMORE daughter of Samuel and Betsey was born 11 April 1799

Elinor PARKER daughter of Elijah and Elenor was born 4 May 1799

William CALLAWAY was born 27 August 1799

William Smith COLLINS son of James and Eleanor was born 30 May 1799

Sarah LOW daughter of Levin and Nelley was born 14 May 1799

Sarah Stevens STURGIS daughter of William and Sarah born 7 June 1799

Nancy FOWLER daughter of Robert and Sally was born 19 July 1799

ELijah OWENS son of Joshua and Violeta was baptized 19 January 1800

Ezekiah McINTYRE son of Daniel and Mary was born 9 June 1799

Sally FORBUS son of Joseph and Polly was born 4 February 1800

Sarah Owens THORNS daughter of Stephen and Sarah was born 5 April 1800

Eli HOWARD son of John and Betsey was born 7 December 1800

Ezekiel JENKINS son of Jarvis and Betsey was born 24 September 1799

Thomas David JENKINS son of Levi and Ready was born 25 November 1799

Rhody FREEMAN daughter of P. D. and Sarah was born 4 July 1798

Betsey GRAY daughter of John Houston and Matilda born 4 July 1798

Thomas GRAVNER son of Loudy and Molley was born 6 February 1801

William Winder PRITCHET son of William and Mary was born 3 March 1801

Ezenezer MILLS son of Mary was born 3 December 1801

Polly HULL daughter of Edward was born 18 November 1800

Thomas TULLIPS son of Joshua and Mary was born 15 January 1801

William RALPH son of Charles and Phillis was born 23 February 1801

George DASHIELL son oof James F. and Mary was born 9 June 1798

Sally RENCHER daughter of John was born 10 September 1801

Harrietta Elizabeth AIRES daughter of Littleton and Saly E. was born 22 December 1801

Polly DUNN daughter of Moses and Susanna was born 12 May 1802

John LANDRETH son of William and Margaret BROWN was born in Parish of Stitchill Berwickshire in Scotland 23 May 1765 and came to America in 1788 and married Margret GILLISS widow of Levin and daughter of William NUTTER and Sarah ECELESTON on 2 August 1797

William DASHIELL son of William and Mary died 19 November 1802 in Cape Francois on the Island of Hispanola

Bridget Venables GOSLIN daughter of Levin and Nelly born 7 March 1802

Esther HUMPHRIS daughter of Elijah and Sally was born 19 April 1802

Matty HEARN daughter of Benjamin and Sarah was born 13 December 1802

Aseneth Bradley COLLINS daughter of John and Aseneth was born 14 October 1802

Elias BAYLEY son of Bordwine and Matty was born 15 April 1802

Peggy HUMPHRISS daughter of Thomas and Molley was born 12 April 1802

John HULL son of Barthingham and Sally was born 8 March 1803

Nelly RUKE daughter of Sovereing and Polly was born 2 October 1802

Joseph WALKER son of John and Margret was born 15 January 1803

Mary Ann LOWES daughter of Tubman and Anne was born 21 March 1803 and baptized 26 June by Rev. William STONE

William Francis DASHIELL son of Ichabod and Priscilla was born 10 March 1803

William HENRY son of John and Rebeckah was born 25 April 1803

Elizabeth Love Turpen PHILIPS daughter of James H. and Rebecka was born 29 September 1802

Leigah TALAR son of John and Ann was born 3 April 1802

John ONEY son of Ephraim and Margret was born 4 June 1801

Easter Sarah Ann Wright HITCHENS daughter of Joseph and Polly was born 7 January 1802

Thomas FOWLER son of Robert and Sarah was born 29 August 1802

Alexander S. EVANS son of James and Betty was born 13 May 1803

William HILL son of Reuben H. and Polly was born 19 December 1802

Elizabeth Esther Ann STANFORD daughter of Col. Clement and Ann was born 26 February 1803

Mathias DASHIELL son of Henry and Elizabeth was born 27 December 1802

Thomas DULANY son of Henry and Rhody was born 1 April 1804

Levin Littleton Gale WEBB son of John and Hetty was born 29 Jan. 1804

Elizabeth Frances COLLIER daughter of Robert and Cathrine was born 11 February 1804

Royston Covington WEATHERLY son of William and Polly born 4 March 1804

Flosa CANTWELL daughter of James and Frankey was born 1 November 1802

Levin Handy JOHNSON son of Clement and Rebecca was born 10 March 1804

Sary Anne WALTER daughter of Benjamin and Jane was born 26 Jan. 1804

Zippa BEDSWORTH daughter of William and Nelly was born 23 January 1804

Henry Smith MURPHY son of Isaac and Elizabeth born 1 February 1804

Levi Wilmer PHILLIPS son of Richard and Priscilla born 16 May 1804

Ebenezer DISHAROON son of Ebenezer and Hetty was born 26 April 1804

Arthur TULLY son of Benjamin and Anne was born 12 December 1803

Amelia Mary Anne TURNER daughter of William and Lina was born 19 October 1803

Maria HAYMAN daughter of Johnson and Esther was born 21 March 1804

Thomas JONES son of John and Martha was born 22 April 1804

William CROCKETT son of John and Nancy was born 23 October 1803

William Littleton AIRES son of Littleton and Sally born 22 Dec. 1803

Sarah Anne ADAMS daughter of John and Anne was born 29 December 1803

James TWILLY son of Robert and Nancy was born 30 March 1804

Getty GOSLEE daughter of Levin and Nelly was born 26 December 1803

Leah Elizabeth Jane CROCKETT daughter of Levin and Sally was born 9 April 1804

Sally Rencher HITCH daughter of Thomas and Molly was born 22 March 1804

Mary Anne SEBREASE daughter of William and Nancy was born 15 June 1804

Lovea ADAMS daughter of Nancy was born 27 November 1803

Richard GOSLLEE daughter of John and Elenor was born 30 December 1803

Thomas PARSONS son of George and Prissy was born 11 October 1802

Mary WALTER daughter of William and Priscilla was born 5 May 1803

Henry DASHIELL son of Henry and Jane was born 3 September 1803

Isaac PHILLIPS son of Roger and Rebecca was born February 1804

Elizabeth DASHIELL daughter of Thomas and Ann was born 24 July 1803

William George Henry JONES son of Wm. and Prissy born 11 December 1802

Whitty McClemmy GILLIS and Thomas Henry GILLIS sons of Ezekiel M. and Sally were born 3 November 1802

Leah Dorman WALKER daughter of Sherman and Molly born 10 July 1803

Priscilla RALPH daughter of James and Mary was born 9 June 1803

Magear BENNETT son of Levin and Elizabeth was born 25 April 1803

Ebenezer MEZICK son of Aaron and Anne was born 17 January 1803

John Twilly HOPKINS son of Richard and Elizabeth born 8 August 1803

Nancy HULL daughter of Edward and Sinea was born 20 May 1803

James HOWARD son of Louder and Betty was born 21 March 1804

Sally BRADLEY daughter of John and Betty was born 22 December 1803

Littleton PARSONS son of Jordan and Leah was born 30 June 1803

Patience Warrington KILLUM daughter of Wm. and Hetty born 31 May 1803

Robert Daugherty ROBERTSON son of John and Betsy was born 1 Oct. 1803

Nelly HOWARD daughter of Joseph and Elizabeth born 30 December 1803

John Tubman LEATHEBURY son of John and Sally was born 24 December 1802

Levin WRIGHT son of William and Nancy was born 15 July 1803

Anne HYNSON daughter of Charles and Anne was born 3 February 1803

Mary Anne HUFFINGTON daughter of John and Nelly born 31 October 1803

Juliannah NEWTON daughter of Nathan C. and Peggy born 10 March 1801

Levin BENNETT son of Joshua and Polly was born 18 January 1804

Mark COOK son of John and Sally was born 27 January 1804

George Washington CAUDRY son of Covington and Ann born 4 October 1803

Sarah ELLIS daughter of Elijah and Sarah was born 7 September 1803

Samuel Hull WALTER son of James L. and Betty was born 28 November 1803

Robert Peregrine LEATHERBURY son of Robert and ELiz. born 13 Nov.1803

Isaac GILES son of William and Jane was born 29 February 1804

Louisa SERMON daughter of Isaac and Betty was born 9 July 1802

Samuel ILES son of Samuel and Elenor was born 10 December 1803

Harriot CROCKETT daughter of Shiles and Anne was born 3 January 1804

Nelly FORBUS daughter of Joseph and Polly was born 10 September 1803

Mary Ann MITCHELL daughter of Thomas was born 20 February 1804

Rebecca KNOALS daughter of William and ELizabeth born 21 January 1804

David VANCE son of George and Martha was born 17 November 1801

Nancy VANCE daughter of George and Martha was born 30 December 1803

Leah Dashiell BAYLY daughter of Samuel and Nancy was born 1 Dec. 1803

Jesse Green COLLINS son of Benjamin and Mary was born 10 August 1803

Zepporah Humphriss NICHOLSON daughter of James and Ann was born 19
September 1803

Catherine MEZICK daughter of Joel and Sally was born 8 November 1803

Nancy TULL daughter of Samuel and Nancy was born 1 October 1803

William Cooper MELSON son of Benjamin and Ebby was born 1 October 1803

Mary RUSSUM daughter of William and Nelly was born 6 May 1803

Bridget RITCHIE daughter of James and Esther was born 9 August 1804

Hannah Hearn HALL daughter of Samuel and Hetty was born 13 Sept.1804

Gertrude D. JENKINS daughter of David and Rebecca born 22 June 1804

Ann Maria JONES daughter of Daniel and Nancy was born 17 April 1804

William Edward WATERS son of Edward and Hannah was born 3 May 1804

Sarah E. B. HUFFINGTON daughter of James and Elinor born 24 Aug.1804

Elizabeth Covington BOUNDS daughter of William and Zippa was born 7 July 1804

Mitchel DASHIELL son of Robert and Mary was born 1 May 1804

Sarah Ann BAYLEY daughter of Henry E. and Sarah born 11 August 1804

James PRITCHARD son of William and Mary was born 21 October 1804

Noah HEARN son of Spencer and Betsy was born 19 August 1804

Joshua JACKSON son of Elihu and Peggy was born 1 September 1804

George Eenezer Robert Jefferson COLLIER son of Ebenezer and Betty was born 9 June 1804

Mary Elizabeth COVINGTON daughter of Phillip and Margaret was born 26 February 1805

Jane Elenor ROBERTSON daughter of Wm. and Esther was born 4 March 1805

William COX son of James and Priscilla was born 3 January 1805

Edward James DASHIELL son of James and Nelly was born 22 December 1804

Levin SMITH son of Elijah and Sally was born 23 March 1805

Nancy ROBERTSON daughter of John and Betty was born 27 January 1805

George Louis AIRES son of Littleton and Sally was born 3 April 1805

Dennis FOUNTAIN son of Thomisson and Nelly was born 8 May 1805

James English RALPH son of Charles and Phillis born 19 February 1805

Mary Weatherly DENNIS daughter of Zadock and Nelly born 2 Feb. 1805

George PHILLIPS son of Joshua and Mary was born 25 November 1802

William WILLIAMS son of John and Molly was born 10 December 1804

Clara INSLEY daughter of Denwood and Betsey was born 11 May 1805

Shadrack DASHIELL son of George was born 28 December 1805

Sarah Matilda Stewart EVANS daughter of James and Betsy was born 9 March 1805

Mary Nichols McCluer DASHIELL daughter of Henry and Jane was born 31 January 1805

Ebenezer Cottman PHILLIPS son of James and Matilda born 8 January1805

Polly GOSLEE daughter of Louder and Betty was born 15 April 1805

Betty ADKINS daughter of David was born 10 April 1805

Anne Mariah PHILLIPS daughter of James and Rebecca born 22 Dec. 1804

Charlotte WINSOR daughter of William and Rellurah born 3 March 1804

Samuel Twilly MORE son of William and Ann was born 11 March 1805

Elijah ELLIS son of Joseph and Sarah was born 7 January 1805

Jane Elizabeth Bridget WAINRIGHT daughter of Levin and Esther was born 14 March 1805

Isaac DORMAN son of George and Rachel was born 24 May 1805

Thomas Wilmer BRITTINGHAM son of Becca was born 13 October 1804

Isaac BAYLEY son of Thomas and Sarah was born 14 June 1805

Mary HILL daughter of Rheubin and Mary was born 27 December 1804

Thomas Jefferson COLLIER son of George and Martha born 27 June 1804

Elizabeth Smith TRADER daughter of Henry and Sally born 25 April 1805

Jane Dorman WALKER daughter of Merrican and Molly born 13 April 1805

Hiram Bell COOPER son of William and Peggy was born 19 August 1805

Jesse LARMORE son of Laramore and Polly was born 18 May 1805

Hetty WRIGHT daughter of Thomas and Nancy was born 19 March 1805

James Howard BAYLEY son of Mathias and Peggy was born 26 Feb. 1805

George FLINT son of William and Tempy was born 19 July 1801

Maria FLINT daughter of William and Tempy was born 1 July 1804

George Handy NICHOLSON son of John and Mary born 22 September 1805

James Trader HENRY son of George and Patience was born 25 Jan. 1805

Benjmain BRUINGTON son of William and Boza was born 6 January 1805

William HULL son of Edward and Sinah was born 30 March 1805

John Venables HUMPHRISS son of Elijah and Sarah born 13 March 1805

Sarah PARKER daughter of William was born 14 December 1804

Joseph PHILLIPS son of Joshua and Mary was born 1 April 1805

Margaret TWILLY daughter of Robert and Nancy was born 23 May 1805

William Thomas Waters HOLBROOK son of Samuel and Jane was born 10 April 1804

James Robins LANGSDALL son of John and Elenor was born 7 July 1805

Hetty OWENS daughter of Isaac and Betty was born 20 March 1805

Sarah Handy NICHOLSON daughter of James and Mary born 13 February 1805

Benjamin Stone HEARN son of William and Polly was born 14 April 1805

Elizabeth Esther Ann STANFORD daughter of Clement and Anne was born 26 February 1803

Mary Eunice Priscilla STANFORD daughter of Clement and Anne was born 19 November 1804

Henrietta Isabella STANFORD daughter of Clement and Anne was born 11 April 1807

Martin BOWLS son of Martin and Peggy was born 21 September 1804

Colian OWENS daughter of Jonathan and Leah was born 4 July 1804

Thomas Evans DASHIELL son of Ichabod and Priscilla born 28 Sep. 1805

Thomas AIRES son of George and Betsy was born 27 October 1805

Betsy SMITH daughter of Edward H. and Eleanor born 13 February 1805

George Washington JACKSON son of Henry Langsdale and Elizabeth was born 1 November 1805

George Washington MITCHELL son of Thomas and Nancy born 29 Feb. 1805

Mary Ann Elizabeth ENSLEY daughter of William and Delilah was born 30 October 1805

Betsy Jackson LEONARD daughter of John and Sarah born 16 August 1805

Nelly Moore HUFFINGTON daughter of John and Nelly born 23 October 1805

Jordan PARSONS son of George and Prisey was born 29 January 1805

Sarah H. HORSEY daughter of John and Mary was born 9 November 1805

Richard BODLEY son of Richard and Rachel was born 15 September 1805

Gatty Franklin CULVER daughter of Levin and Elizabeth born 31 Aug. 1805

Polly DAILY daughter of Samuel and Molly was born 14 October 1805

Francis MEZICK son of Aaron and Anna was born 20 June 1805

Simon Wilmer BRADLEY son of John and Betsy was born 1 June 1805

Sarah TALL daughter of Samuel and Nancy was born 23 September 1805

Betsy DAVIS daughter of John and Polly was born 6 June 1805

Joanna HEARN daughter of William and Sally was born 7 August 1805

Matilda Elizabeth TULL daughter of Brittingham and Sally was born 22 September 1805

Perry Robertson BRADLEY son of Levin and Hannah born 1 September 1805

Daniel FOOKES son of Thomas and Leah was born 7 July 1805

Ephraim COLLINS son of Benjamin and Mary was born 23 May 1805

Peter Dashiell WEATHERLY son of James and Betsy was born 8 August 1805

ELiza Ann Jones DASHIELL daughter of George and Eleanor was born 18 December 1805

Mary GREEN daughter of Asa and Elizabeth was born 31 October 1805

Louisa MEZICK daughter of Joel and Sarah was born 29 October 1805

Sarah Dorman GREEN daughter of Zadock and Eleanor born 11 Sep. 1805

Beauchamp HOWARD son of Joseph and Betsy was born 4 November 1805

Harvey HAYMAN son of Johnson and Esther was born 15 November 1805

Britanny S. WRIGHT daughter of William and Nancy born 15 November 1805

Mary Ann VENABLES daughter of Richard and Sally born 2 February 1805

Sally M. ACWORTH daughter of Samuel and Ketturah born 19 October 1805

John B. HASTY son of James and Allefair was born 16 August 1805

Henry PHILLIPS son of James and Polly was born 14 October 1805

Robert PHILLIPS son of Day and Peggy was born 29 November 1805

Polly BAYLEY daughter of Matthias and Peggy was born 31 October 1806

Nelly H. BENNETT daughter of Levin and Elizabeth born 6 April 1806

Rosanna STORKS daughter of Phillip and Mary was born 2 December 1806

William HALL son of Samuel and Hetty was born 12 October 1806

William ROBERTS son of Joshua B. and Betsy was born 21 February 1806

Robert AIRES son of Littleton and Sally E. was born 16 July 1806

Eleanor ROBERTSON daughter of John and Betsy was born 15 April 1806

Rider Winder WILSON son of William and Nancy was born 19 December 1806

Charlotte W. WILSON daughter of William and Nancy born 19 Dec. 1806

Mary MOORE daughter of William and Ann was born 15 December 1806

Major H. WINSOR son of Isaac and Mary was born 12 August 1806

Alford Smith WRIGHT son of Thomas and Nancy was born 28 November 1806

Anna HENRY daughter of John and Rebecca was born 7 March 1806

Joseph HUMPHREYS son of Joshua and Elizabeth was born 29 November 1806

Elihu JACKSON son of John and Nelly was born 8 December 1806

William Cottman KELLAM son of William and Hetty was born 28 Jan. 1806

Nancy Brown ROBERTSON daughter of Samuel and Emily was born 8 Oct.1806

Priscilla COVINGTON daughter of Phillip and Peggy born 25 June 1806

Martha W. AIRES daughter of George and Betsy was born 28 August 1806

John Turpin VENABLES son of Joseph and Sally was born 3 March 1806

Eliza SELBY daughter of Robert and Leah was born 3 January 1806

John Bayley BODLEY son of Elisha and Charlotte born 25 October 1806

Henrietta DASHIELL daughter of Levin and Mary was born 18 May 1806

William WALLER son of James and Elizabeth was born 26 December 1806

Amelia DASHIELL daughter of Robert and Mary was born 2 September 1806

Rebecca SIMS daughter of Smith and Sally was born 9 September 1806

Josiah Bayley MILLER son of John and Sarah was born 27 April 1806

Isaac D. JONES son of Benjamin and Priscilla was born 10 November 1806

Mary E. HOPKINS daughter of Matthias D. and Nelly was born 13 May 1806

Eliza Ann BAYLEY daughter of Bordwine and Matilda born 23 October 1806

Whittington COX son of Thomas and Sally was born 16 January 1806

Joshua Cottman PHILLIPS son of Richard and Priscilla born 9 April 1806

Ann PHILLIPS daughter of Charles and Sarah was born 23 January 1806

Thomas D. H. WHITE son of Gowan and Biddy was born 13 March 1806

Levin FURBUS son of Joseph and Polly was born 24 January 1806

Jane BOUNDS daughter of William and Zippy was born 2 February 1806

Noah Humphreys JENKINS son of David and Rebecca was born 19 March 1806

James JONES son of George and Peggy was born 29 January 1806

William Hitch WEATHERLY son of Peregrine L. and Peggy was born 30 March 1806

Henrietta CROCKETT daughter of Shiles and Ann born 28 February 1806

William BIRD son of Thomas and Sarah was born 15 February 1806

George E. LARMORE son of John and Peggy was born 25 September 1806

Hosea HENRY son of James and Sarah was born 26 January 1806

James K. HEARN son of Thomas and Sarah was born 4 September 1806

John H. PARSONS son of Jordan and Leah was born 15 June 1806

Henry D. WRIGHT son of Isaac and Henny was born 11 February 1806

Edwin DASHIELL son of Arthur and Esthr was born 21 April 1806

Henry DASHIELL son of Thomas and Elizabeth was born 24 February 1806

Nancy W. WALLER daughter of Jonathan and Rachel born 7 January 1806

James Robert John Mc Clester FOUNTAIN son of Henry and Betsy was born 30 December 1806

Nancy KNOLES daughter of William and Elizabeth was born 28 Feb. 1806

James ELLIS son of William and Amey was born 5 November 1806

Eleanor Leatherbury Bluet RENCHER daughter of Thomas and Priscilla was born 1 December 1806

Thomas D. JILES son of William and Gainer was born 29 January 1807

John L. DUN son of Moses and Suckey was born 12 January 1806

Nelly Bennet BAYLY daughter of Wm. and Aeseaneath born 23 Feb. 1807

Samuel B. GOSLEE son of Loudy and Betsy was born 21 February 1807

George LOWE son of Samuel and Ruth was born 4 March 1807

Thomas FOOKS son of Thomas and Leah was born 4 April 1807

Isaac HOPKINS son of Isaac and Martha was born 4 April 1807

Amelia TRADER daughter of Henry and Sally was born 9 February 1807

Charles V. CROCKETT son of Levin and Sarah was born 19 June 1807

Elford WALTER son of Richard and Rachel was born 11 April 1807

Jonthan W. GILLISS son of Ezechel and Ann was born 10 March 1807

Catherine ACWORTH daughter of Samuel and Kiturah was born 2 April 1807

Daniel J. DASHIELL son of James and Nelly was born 16 March 1807

Henry DASHIELL son of Thomas and Elizabeth was born 4 February 1806

Thomas Cooper BAILY son of Thomas and Betsy was born 10 February 1807

Thomas JENKINS son of Jarvis and Betsy was born 10 September 1807

Beard Robertson PHILLIPS son of William and Elizabeth was born 17 April 1806

Nancy C. HENRY daughter of George and Patience was born 2 April 1807

Cale R. HORNER daughter of Levin and Sarah was born 14 February 1807

Josiah D. MILLS son of Isaac and Elizabeth was born 5 March 1807

George LARMORE son of Samuel and Elizabeth was born 14 January 1807

Patty BARCLAY daughter of John and Polly was born 20 February 1807

Catharine W. BENSON daughter of Benjamin and Peggy born 19 Nov. 1806

Susan PHIPPS son of Absolem and Nancy was born 7 January 1806

Archelaus HUMPHRESS son of Elijah and Sarah was born 23 April 1807

John M. PHILLIPS son of Benjamin and Sally was born 4 March 1806

James COX son of James and Priscilla was born 1 January 1807

Dnaiel PHILLIPS son of Joshua and Mary was born 22 March 1807

Noah JACKSON son of Elihu and Peggy was born 3 November 1807

Jane DASHIELL daughter of William and Mary was born 1 September 1806

Mary ENGLIS daughter of Levin and Sarah was born 1 May 1807

Sally PHILLIPS daughter of Joshua and Polly was born 16 January 1807

Thomas RALPH son of James and Mary was born 17 January 1806

Ebenezer TAYLOR son of Ebenezer and Betty was born 3 January 1807

Rosey W. ROSE daughter of William and Elinor was born 10 February 1807

Susan HILL daughter of Rheuben H. and Polly was born 7 April 1807

Mary and Ann DRISKELL daughters of Aaron and Jane were born 15 January 1807

Betsey Winsor JOHNSON daughter of Clement and Rebecca born 10 Feb.1807

Susan Jones DUN daughter of Richard and Prsicilla born 22 April 1806

George Ballard LANGSDALE son of Joshua and Matilda born 27 Nov. 1806

Nancy TOADVINE daughter of John and Sally was born 2 May 1806

Joseph Humphress FLINT son of William and Tempy was born 30 March 1807

Leaven COOPER son of William and Peggy was born 23 February 1807

James RUSSELL son of James and Mary was born 8 April 1805

Sarah RUSSELL daughter of James and Mary was born 22 May 1808

Charlotte FLETCHER daughter of Levin and Sarah born 15 September 1806

Mary Priscilla Evans DASHIELL daughter of Nicholas and Elizabeth J. was born 13 April 1807

Polly Gray COX daughter of Thomas and Sally was born 18 September 1807

Sarah Jean and Eliza Ann COLLIER daughters of George and Martha were born 3 December 1807

Joseph TWILLY son of Robert and Nancy was born 27 November 1807

Josiah Thomas Dashiell BAYLY son of Samuel and Nancy born 5 Feb. 1808

Sarah GRAY daughter of John and Margaret was born 23 January 1807

Eliza Jackson PHILLIPS daughter of Richard and Levina was born 22 February 1807

George PARSONS son of George and Priscilla was born 23 August 1807

Milcah Farrington PHILLIPS daughter of Day and Peggy born 28 June 1807

Thomas Dashiell EVANS son of James and Betsy was born 14 June 1807

Betsy PHILLIPS daughter of Benjamin and Sally was born 11 May 1808

Ebby Cupper BRADLEY daughter of John and Betsy was born 15 March 1808

George TULL son of Samuel and Nancy was born 20 June 1807

Mary Ann Leatherbury BOUNDS daughter of William and Zeporah was born 22 December 1807

Edward HULL son of Brittingham and Sally was born 29 September 1807

Richard Ellensworth LARMORE son of Elijah and Mary was born 9 Oct.1807

Esther Hitch ELLISS daughter of Elijah and Sarah was born 25 Jan.1808

John ROBERTSON son of John and Betsy was born 20 December 1807

Levi Washington JOHSNON son of John and Elizabeth born 1 February 1808

Delilah ENSLEY daughter of William and Libby was born 16 January 1808

William DUN son of Moses and Susan was born 5 November 1807

Noah HOPKINS son of Samuel and Jemimah was born 28 October 1807

Eliza VENABLES daughter of Joseph and Sally was born 6 November 1807

Levin Phillips TWILLY son of Robert and Nancy was born 9 Jan. 1808

Sarah Elizabeth MOORE daughter of Wm. and Rebecca born 22 October 1807

Francis MITCHELL son of Thomas and Nancy was born 28 June 1807

Robert Napoleon DASHIELL son of Peter and Priscilla born 15 Oct. 1807

Isaac Richard DUN son of Richard and Priscilla born 6 September 1807

Alcey Elizabeth Bradley ROBERTSON daughter of Samuel and Amelia was born 7 December 1808

Elizabeth Esther Ann JONES daughter of William and Amelia was born 8 April 1807

Peter Owings VANCE son of George and Hetty was born 3 September 1807

Mary Ann Records BYRD daughter of Thomas and Sarah born 14 Nov. 1807

William Bradley NICHOLSON son of Joseph and Polly born 18 October 1807

Noah PARKER son of William and Hannah was born 11 March 1807

Lemuel RENCHER son of Samuel and Elizabeth was born 5 August 1807

Mary Ann HENRY daughter of James and Sarah was born 23 March 1808

James MALCUM son of Tubman and Elizabeth was born 21 November 1807

Esther Nicholson WRIGHT daughter of William and Nancy was born 5 November 1807

Mary Ann Elizabeth ELZEY daughter of Arnold was born 28 January 1808

Shiles Crockett SEABREASE son of William and Nancy born 15 April 1808

John Twilfare DARBY son of Thomas and Sally was born 27 March 1808

Kendle Batson HASTING son of Joseph and Nelly born 13 September 1801

Ichabod HEARN son of Spencer and Betsy was born 9 April 1808

Henry WHITE son of Joseph and Polly was born 20 December 1807

Mary Ann LANKFORD daughter of William H.and Lydia born 21 July 1807

Nathan P. PARSONS son of Levin and Hannah was born 29 October 1806

Betsy HITCH daughter of Robert and Nelly was born 22 May 1807

William Pitt WAINRIGHT son of Levin and Hetty was born 24 May 1807

Hester CROCKETT daughter of Shiles and Anna was born 22 May 1808

Maria Elizabeth HOPKINS daughter of William and Leah born 19 Feb.1807

Levin PRICE son of Kibble and Sarah was born 29 August 1807

John Schoolfield WILSON son of Henry and Catharine born 23 May 1807

Martha MEZICK daughter of Joel and Sarah was born 22 January 1808

Joshua Leanord NIBBLET son of William and Nancy born 25 November 1807

Phillip COVINGTON son of Phillip and Margaret born 5 January 1808

William Daley SMITH son of Elijah and Sally was born 30 January 1808

Levin King HORNER son of Levin and Sarah was born 20 February 1808

Uriah LARMORE son of Jacob and Molly was born September 10 1807

William KEMP son of John and Elizabeth was born 20 May 1807

Benjamin COTTMAN son of Benjamin and Susan was born 24 December 1807

Nelly GOSLEE daughter of John and Nelly was born 29 December 1807

Carolina Leah Matilda STANFORD daughter of Clement and Ann was born in
Vienna Dorchester County 1 April 1809 and died 7 October 1810

Tubman LOWES son of Henry and Esther married Elizabeth Birkhead BOND
daughter of Thomas and Elizabeth of Calvert County 9 April 1789

Esther Tubman LOWES daughter of Tubman and Elizabeth born 29 Jan. 1790

Tubman LOWES son of Tubman and Elizabeth was born 17 October 1791

Benson Bond LOWES son of Tubman and Elizabeth was born 2 February 1793
and baptized on 11 March 1793

79

Elizabeth LOWES daughter of Tubman and Elizabeth was born 25 November 1794 and baptized 4 April 1795

Dorothy LOWES daughter of Tubman and Elizabeth was born 3 January 1797 and died on 1 October 1797. Baptized 22 January 1797.

Mary Henry LOWES daughter of Tubman and Elizabeth was born 24 November 1799 and died 5 December 1799. Baptized 1 December 1799

Elizabeth B. LOWES wife of Tubman died 28 November 1799

Tubman LOWES son of Henry and Esther married Ann HITCH daughter of Joshua and Mary of Somerset County on 11 March 1801

Mary Ann LOWES daughter of Tubman and Ann was born 21 March 1803 and baptized 26 June 1803

John Dashiell STANFORD son of Clement and Anne was born 13 May 1811 and died 28 July 1812

Margaret Eleanor STANFORD daughter of Clement and Anne was born 24 September 1813

George D. WALTER married Mary B. WATERS 28 September 1814

Margaret ELizabeth Dashiell WALTER daughter of George D. and Mary was born 11 September 1815

George D. ATKINSON married Henrietta RUSSUM 1 March 1815

George Sydenham ATKINSON son of George D. and Henrietta was born 5 January 1816

Mary Priscilla ATKINSON daughter of George D. and Henrietta was born 12 January 1817

Sarah Esther Priscilla WALTER daughter of George D. and Mary was born 14 June 1817

Richard Clement Sidney STANFORD son of Clement and Anne was born 8 March 1816

Harriet Tubman WALTER daughter of George D. and Mary born 24 June 1819

George Dashiell WALTER son of George D. and Mary born 1 October 1821

Esther Ann Dashiell WALTER daughter of Robert and Margaret was born 31 December 1816

Robert WALTER son of Robert and Mary was born 12 April 1818

Margaret Elizabeth WALTER daughter of Robert and Margaret was born 8 September 1819

Mary Jacobs WALTER daughter of Robert and Margaret born 8 April 1821

Daniel James WALTER son of Robert and Margaret born 28 December 1822

Sarah Elizabeth JONES daughter of Levin and Matilda was born 24 January 1824

Priscilla Jones WALTER daughter of Robert and Margaret was born 1 October 1824

ELiza Henrietta STEWART daughter of Robert and Nancy died 28 May 1826 age 8 months.

Bridget Jane WALTER daughter of Robert and Margaret was born 8 December 1826

Capt. George D. ATKINSON died 6 October 1824 age 48 years, 4 days.

Robert S. GRAHAM son of Phillip and Nancy died 5 January 1832

Hester Hurley STEWART daughter of Robert and Nancy died 18 August 1832, age 8 months.

James W. DASHIELL late vestry man of Stepney Parish died on 15 October 1832.

Col. Isaac Atkinson died 28 February 1833 age 68.

Mrs. Priscilla ATKINSON wife of Col. Isaac died 10 July 1833

The Rt. Rev. Bishop WHITE DD of Pennsylvania and Presiding Bishop of the Protestant Episcopal Church died on 17 July 1836. age 89. In the 50th year of his episcopal consecration.

The Right Rev. William M. STONE DD Bishop of the Protestant Episcopal Church in Maryland died on 26 February 1838, age 58 years.

Capt. Jesse HUGHS died 29 November 1838 at his residence near White Haven, age 70 years, 9 months.

Eba JONES daughter of Thomas J. and Rose E. was born in Tyaskin 27 October 1883 and baptized at St. Mary's Church 27 April 1884

Ora Lee WILLING was born on 19 June 1881 at Nanticoke Point daughter of John W. and Georgianna and baptized 9 November 1884 at St. Mary's Church in Tyaskin

John W. Harrison WILLING son of John W. and Georgianna was born 4 February 1883 and baptized 9 November 1884 at St. Mary's Church

Georgia Anna WINGATE daughter of George E. and Arianna A. was born 4 October 1870 at Wicomico County and baptized at St. Bartholomew's Church, Green Hill on 26 August 1883

Lucy Virginia WALLER daughter of Benjamin Franklin and Fannie E. was born 5 June 1882 and baptized 25 August 1885 at St. Bartholomew's Church at Green Hill.

William Richard KENNERLY was born 5 June 1882 son of William R. W. and Lizzie E. and baptized 26 August 1883 at St. Bartholomew's Church

Wade Hamilton KENNERLY son of William R. W. and Lizzie E. was born 29 February 1880 and baptized 26 August 1883 at St. Bartholomew's Church

Thomas ROSS born 10 July 1882 was born 10 July 1882 and baptized 26 August 1885 at St. Bartholomew's Church

Thomas Franklin RIDER son of James Franklin and Kate N. born May 1881 was baptized 26 August 1885 at St. Bartholomew's Church

Mary Elizabeth RIDER daughter of James Franklin and Kate N. was born June 1884 and baptized 26 August 1885 at St. Bartholomew's Church

John Walter Nelson JONES son of Thomas J. Jones and Rose E. was born at Tyaskin on 26 May 1885 was baptized 30 August 1885 at St. Mary's Chapel, in Tyaskin.

Bertha Delmay INSLEY daughter of Samuel Hicks and Alexine was born in the Trappe District Wicomico County 16 January 1883 and was baptized on 25 August 1885 at St. Bartholomew's Church at Green Hill.

Lizzie May BRADLEY daughter of James and Josephine born in the Trappe District on 4 October 1884 and baptized on 24 August 1886 at St. Bartholomew's Church

Myrtie Irene BRADLEY daughter of James and Josephine was baptized 24 August 1886 at St. Bartholomew's Church

Rufus Marion DASHIELL son of Levin J. and Martha W. born at Green Hill on 30 June 1869 was baptized 22 May 1877 at St. Bartholomew's Church

Amos Thomas DASHIELL son of Levin J. and Martha W. was born 23 December 1872 and baptized on 22 May 1877 at St. Bartholomew's Church

Mary Lizzie DASHIELL daughter of Levin J. and Martha W. born 13 July

1874 was baptized at St. Bartholomew's Church 22 May 1877

Eva Blanche DASHIELL daughter of Levin J. and Martha W. was born 24 December 1876 and baptized 22 May 1877 St. Bartholomew's Church

Edith May DASHIELL daughter of above was born 4 June 1878 and baptized on 22 May 1887 at St. Bartholomew's Church

Sallie Gertrude JONES was born 20 October 1864 and baptized on 22 May 1887 at St. Bartholomew's Church

Olive Marie JONES daughter of Levlin and Sallie J. was born at Mt. Vernon on 28 January 1886 and baptized at St. Bartholomew's Church on 26 June 1887.

Hattie Eliza DASHIELL daughter of Levin was born at Green Hill on 16 September 1882 and baptized on 26 June 1887

Harry Lee DASHIELL son of Levin J. and Martha W. was born 13 December 1884 at Green Hill and baptized on 26 June 1887

Pratt Dashiell PHILLIPS son of Isaac Thomas and Helen born near Quantico on 10 March 1887 was baptized 20 July 1887 at St. Bartholomew's

James Littleton LEATHERBURY son of Levin K. and Priscilla born near Grace Church on 12 February 1832 was baptized on 7 August 1887 at St. Bartholomew's Church

Charles Lemuel LEATHERBURY son of James L. and Matilda Frances was born at White Haven on 26 May 1861 and baptized 7 August 1887 at St. Bartholomew's

James Hyland DASHIELL son of Levin J. and Martha W. born near White Haven on 23 February 1867 was baptized on 7 August 1887 at St. Bartholomew's.

Margaret Ellen JONES daughter of John Wesley and Helen PORTER born at Tyaskin on 14 January 1862 was baptized on 21 March 1887 at St. Mary's in Tyaskin.

William Benjamin MESSICK son of W. F. and Henrietta HOPKINS born at Tyaskin on 6 August 1862 was baptized on 31 March 1889 at St. Mary's

Robert Fulton WALLER son of B. Franklin and Fannie WINGATE born near Green Hill on 12 December 1886 was baptized on 28 August 1889 at St. Bartholomew's

Oscar Wilmer RIALL son of John Hilary and Ella F. born at Tyaskin on 16 June 1888 was baptized 19 March 1890 at St. Mary's Church

William Benjamin MESSICK age 27 was confirmed at St. Mary's in Tyaskin on 13 April 1889

Louella KENNERLY age 18 was confirmed at St. Mary' 13 April 1889

Margaret Ellen JONES age 27 was confirmed at St. Mary' 13 April 1889

Thomas J. JONES age 23 married Rosa E. WALTER age 27 daughter of Sallie at Tyaskin 17 June 1883, St. Mary' Church

William Frank LANGRELL age 27 married Jennie L. COVINGTON age 21 on 11 December 1883 at the brides home in Tyaskin

Otis LLOYD age 21 son of Ralph of White Haven married Hettie E. Leatherbury age 17 daughter of L. LEATHERBURY on 16 December 1884

John R. D. LANKFORD married Sallie A. WINGATE daughter of George on 22 December 1886 at Green Hill Church

Miss Maris WALTER age 83 of Nanticoke Point, died of paralysis on 20 August 1883 and was buried on 22 August 1883 St. Mary' church yard in Tyaskin

John RIALL of Tyaskin died 14 April 1884 of general debility and was buried on 17 April 1884 St. Mary's Church yard

Mrs. Eliza J. DASHIELL age 73 of Somerset County died on 30 Novembr 1886 of general debility and was buried on 1 December 1886 in St. Bartholomew's church yard.

John DOUGHERTY was buried on 28 November 1887 in St. Mary's churchyard

Miss Eugenia RIALL age 24 of Baltimore died on 8 October 1889 of Malaria and was buried on 11 October 1889 at Parsons Cemetery in Salisbury Maryland.

CONFIRMATIONS 13 July 1803

Littleton AIRES   age 27
Clement STANFORD age 26
Jesse HUGHES age 36
Sarah HUGHS age 28
Levin BALLARD age 21
Jacob AIRES age 18
Sarah EVANS age 43
John McCLESTER age 60
John DASHIELL
Eleanor DASHIELL age 44
Margaret DONE age 16
Sally BISHOP age 21
George D. ATKINSON age 30
Shiles CROCKETT
Levin CROCKETT age 34
James RITCHIE age 42
Nanney PARE age 19
John JACKSON age 28
Betsy GOSLEE age 21
Elihu JACKSON age 57
Elizabeth RENCHER age 27
John TILGHMAN age 46
Rachael WILSON age 46
Priscilla TRAVERSE age 34
Denny BURK age 36
Elizabeth BURKE age 58
Sarah ELLIS age 35
Ann WRIGHT age 20
Pierce POWELL age 45
Mary HITCH age 39
Sally JONES age 49
Elizabeth GODDART age 22
Keziah DALEY age 50
Nancy GODDART age 47
Nancy RALPH age 33
Eleanor COLLIER age 52
Eleanor BIGLAND age 42
Amelia DISHAROON age 30
Sarah SMITH age 27
Ann TOADVINE age 19
George DASHIELL age 26
Susan COTTMAN age 26
Polly VETRE age 24
Nancy BUTLER age 54
Leanor JONES age 27
Sarah LARMORE age 24
Phillis ROBERTSON age 40
Elizabeth HOBBS age 37
Spencer DAVIS age 59
P. WEATHERLY age 25
Nancy HEARN age 22
Nancy MITCHELL

Benjamin ROBERTS age 24
Elizabeth ROBERTS age 22
Margaret L. DASHIELL age 17
Rose NELSON age 17
Isabella DASHIELL age 18
Amelia AIRES   age 18
Ann DASHIELL b. 22 July 1795
Betsy McCLESTER b. 23 July 1807
Priscilla DASHIELL age 64
Priscilla DASHIELL age 37
Sarah M. DONE age 22
Mary DONE age 20
Nelly FREENEY age 22
Peggy HALES age 16
Silas C. BUSH age 32
ELizabeth RITCHIE age 36
Mary DALY age 30
Susan BENSEN age 44
Ephraim BENSON age 41
Esther WILSON
John BURK age 34
Nancy TILGHMAN age 35
Ann LOW age 20
Alice WEST age 22
Esther LANKFORD age 44
Nancy VINCENT age 39
Keziah NICHOLS age 19
Rhoda TOADVINE age 39
Sally SIMS age 20
Mary JACKSON age 53
Sally RENCHER age 26
Esther CALLIHAM age 65
Molly DISHAROON age 23
Molly BANKS age 45
Betsy MOORE age 27
Betsy FREENEY age 35
Sally LEONARD age 23
Elijah S. SMITH age 67
Mary DORMAN age 57
Milcha VENABLES age 38
Sally SIMS age 24
Leah SMITH age 42
Elizabeth WALTER age 46
Thomas JONES age 35
Sally BANKS age 22
Leah SAVAGE age 21
Thomas RENCHER age 30
Samuel HALL age 33
Charles WEATHERLY age 56
Polly HITCH age 35
John HALE age 58
Ann CROCKETT age 26

85

John LARMORE age 25
Ann BIGLAND age 53
William HEARN age 40
MARY ADKINS age 28
Sally GRAHAM age 26
Joshua HUMPHRISS age 20
Peggy VENABLES age 27
Elizabeth HUMPHRISS age 47
James WALTER age 51
Elizabeth JONES age 18
Mary STONE age 29
Jane COTTMAN age 16
Nelly GUPTON age 17
Nancy DASHIELL age 17
Tubman LOWES age 16
James PARE age 16
Doughty BOUNDS age 41
Sarah VENABLES age 26

Mary NICHOLSON
Mary TURNER age 50
Elizabeth EVANS age 25
Mary BOUNDS age 19
Susana STURGIS age 47
Nancy SEABREASE age 27
Peggy GRAY age 32
Eleanor RUSSUM age 36
Susan JONES age 22
Joseph COTTMAN age 23
Elizabeth STONE age 24
Mary WEATHERLY age 18
Teressa DASHIELL age 19
Benson B. LOWES age 14
George W. JONES age 16
James COVINGTON age 26
Peggy CHAMBERS age 27
Anne R. WALLER age 16

< continue on next page >

90

www.ingramcontent.com/pod-product-compliance
Lightning Source LLC
LaVergne TN
LVHW051703080426
835511LV00017B/2705